A Priceless View

A Priceless View

MY SPIRITUAL HOMECOMING

DEIRDRE CORNELL

ORBIS BOOKS

Maryknoll, New York 10545

Founded in 1970, Orbis Books endeavors to publish works that enlighten the mind, nourish the spirit, and challenge the conscience. The publishing arm of the Maryknoll Fathers and Brothers, Orbis seeks to explore the global dimensions of the Christian faith and mission, to invite dialogue with diverse cultures and religious traditions, and to serve the cause of reconciliation and peace. The books published reflect the views of their authors and do not represent the official position of the Maryknoll Society. To learn more about Maryknoll and Orbis Books, please visit our website at www.maryknoll.org.

Library of Congress Cataloging-in-Publication Data

Cornell, Deirdre.
    A priceless view : my spiritual homecoming / Deirdre Cornell.
      p.   cm.
    ISBN 1-57075-489-6 (pbk.)
    1. Cornell, Deirdre. 2. Catholics – New York (State) – Newburgh –
Biography. I. Title.
BX4705.C7775 A3 2004
282'.092 – dc21

                                                      2003009842

for Kenney, of course

Contents

Acknowledgments

Someone wrote, With so many debts to acknowledge, one feels not poor, but rich.

First, to my brother, who wandered my childhood with me, and to our parents, who followed the path of their commitment — I love you.

To those who helped me become a woman of faith and a writer: the Grail women, especially the Cornwall team and the Women of the Americas; faculty at Smith College and the Jesuit School of Theology; and Joe and Sally Cunneen, who launched me into writing — blessings upon you.

To those who guided my husband and me in ministry as we found our way in Newburgh: the Presentation Sisters of the Blessed Virgin Mary and parish staff of St. Patrick's Church, Christian Brother Daniel Crimmins of Reaping the Harvest, and Fr. Tomas Bobadilla — peace be with you.

To my *compadres* and *ahijados*, to my neighbors and friends, in Newburgh and on the farms, who in sharing their lives opened a whole new world to me — *qué Dios les recompense*. I have changed some names of living persons and have modified some details, but I have been faithful in describing my experiences and, to the best of my ability, have portrayed the city's past with historical integrity.

To the staff of the archives room of the Newburgh Free Library who facilitated my research, to the generous friends who donated a printer for this project, and to Noell Goldberg and John Eagleson, who edited the manuscript — thank you.

To the publishing crew at Orbis Books, especially Mike Leach and Robert Ellsberg — I appreciate your patience! Good things come to those who wait.

Most importantly, to my husband, whose love of travel brought us together — you are my true home. Without you, Newburgh would have made no sense. To our children, with whom we journey — I hope your father and I can teach you how to find your own place. Don't forget to fasten your seatbelts.

Lastly, thanks to my integration group at Bethany for helping me see that I can leave.

Introduction

Let it be said from the start, so that no subterfuge stand between us, no veil of false piety mask the sad truth: I never wanted to return to Newburgh. When one leaves this dead-end city, one shakes the dust off one's feet in relief and never looks back. Once its young people leave they come home only in disgrace, having failed to achieve the American Dream elsewhere. Like the cynic who asked, "Can anything good come out of Nazareth?" (John 1:46), I have often posed a similar question. What has brought me back here, to these crumbling mansions overlooking the Hudson River in one of the poorest cities of its size in the United States? And like the doubter in the Gospel story who became a disciple, I receive a reply framed as an invitation: "Come and see."

In the exodus that had freed me from this place, I earned a bachelor's degree at a prestigious college that my childhood friends (many of whom did not finish high school) have never heard of. I married a man from the state geographically farthest from here, and we lived for a brief time on the opposite side of the country. The nagging unease I used to feel, as if I were an imposter from the wrong side of the tracks trying to "pass," finally subsided as I studied for a master's degree. With every passing year since my parents moved our family from Newburgh two decades ago, at each increment of time and distance my escape seemed more complete, the felicitous estrangement permanent.

But Newburgh haunted me. In recurring dreams I would find myself again on the wide grassy expanse called the Bluff, where we played as children. Hem brushing the tops of trees, my body, flatly horizontal, skimmed the cliff leading down to the river in an explosion of freedom. I woke with arms and legs tingling, lungs bursting for air. My waking hours too were usurped by unsolicited memories. At unexpected moments a rank, slightly salty smell might transport me to those humid summers on the banks of the Hudson River, its water rich with decomposing matter, its taste strangely metallic. Whenever I see scenes of urban street life in a new city, I remember the gaggle of kids of mixed ages and backgrounds, tearing up the pavement in our bare feet. And as much as I tried to avoid the memory of myself, a skinny cornbraided teenager sampling Southern cooking at our next-door neighbor's house, or devouring corn pie in the basement apartment of the best friend whom I have never seen again, in Newburgh's kitchens I first tasted hospitality.

In seeking glimpses of God's hand at creation, in this country and in others, I have stood in awe before many breathtaking sites of natural beauty. The Hudson River Valley, celebrated by painters, poets, singers, and writers, ranks high among them. But only at this particular bend in the river, just past Storm King Mountain and directly across from Mount Beacon, with Bannerman's Island in plain sight off to the right, do land, water, and sky come together in perfect proportion. Only this panorama, with its varying textures and colors according to season, can satisfy a silent ache that otherwise curls unnoticed around my heart. A sigh waiting to be released, so powerful it can suspend breath. A heartsickness that begs for words.

You see, I must tell you another sad truth: I never wanted to *leave* Newburgh.

YEARS AGO, my father had lost his job for an international interfaith organization after fourteen years (sort of a peace movement version of "downsizing"). Neither of the area's two major employers, International Business Machines (IBM) nor West Point Military Academy, offered viable work for a seasoned activist. Unemployment checks long spent, my father tried substitute teaching and my mother, baby-sitting. After two years of struggling unsuccessfully to get off food stamps and to keep our home, my family was forced to move away.

Since we left very early in the morning, no one came out to say good-bye. The rental van had been packed the night before with our furniture, books, and other belongings and would be driven by a family friend. My mother, brother, and I, with the dog and cat, were to follow in a separate car. (My father had preceded us by several months in order to start the school year at his new teaching job in New Hampshire.) There had been farewell dinners given by neighbors and even a party, during which I sobbed conspicuously, but I had somehow not believed that this day would actually come. The remaining details were taken care of; the final bags of toiletries and odds and ends were stashed into the car. As winter's thin sunlight turned the mountains from a velvety black to a plush purple, we watched the river's steely gray waters from our front porch for the last time.

My exile had begun.

COMING BACK AFTER SO LONG, a grown woman with children of my own, I thought that Newburgh would now offer some familiarity to soothe my long-held grief. But in searching for the past from which to be healed, I cannot find it. The public school where I had attended kindergarten stands boarded up and spray painted, a congregating place for dope dealers. The corner store where we used to buy chips and sweets now specializes in selling *tamales*. Our parish grammar school closed long ago. As I adjust to the city's changes in geography, my internal compass is thrown off.

It is not that the city has been degraded to such a point that it is unrecognizable as the place where I grew up. After all, long before we lived here, Newburgh had acquired an unsavory reputation. My parents were able to buy a house here precisely *because* it was poor. And during my childhood, white flight had already set up invisible borders of suburban and urban segregation, battle lines of racial demarcation. Furthermore, in some ways the city is better off now than it was when we lived here. More social welfare projects and commercial developments serve the city now than when I was young. In a much touted "Renaissance," recently the City Hall and the old Armory building were stunningly renovated, as have been several old mansions and the waterfront area on the river. What troubles me now is the fear that this return offers no balm for my restlessness.

A prodigal daughter who "gathered all [she] had and traveled to a distant country" (Luke 15:13), after so many years I have come back without knowing what to expect. The familiar and the foreign crash into one another like contrary waves. Does the home of my childhood still exist? If so, will I find a welcome there, like the returning heir of the Gospel story? An even more brutal question: Can this battered city be trusted to soothe my bruises from the past? Wanderlust pulses in my blood, vibrant. The *inquietud* (restlessness) awakened during time spent away from here leads me to delve into the city's contradictions. Rapacious, I wander the city's new terrain, gloating over the discovery: fresh landscapes of narrative to be explored.

I had jealously guarded the loss of my first home as if it were a private wound. As I nurse the discipline of attention, that most crucial of faculties, my gaze widens. Now I see that this particular bend of the Hudson, so near and yet so far from Manhattan, houses many who have known such grief. If, as locals claim, Newburgh is home to failures of the American Dream (which was never meant to encompass all Americans, anyway), it is also home to newcomers who have exchanged one brand of poverty for another.

Some have come to start new lives, immigrants whose hearts yearn for other rivers and other mountains but whose children will call Newburgh home. Others will stay just long enough to earn money and then return to their countries of origin. Many will be caught in between. Trapped in the net of necessity, they feed their children on food and stories brought from somewhere else. Will I be stuck here, too? Like their children, I was raised on an inherited ambivalence. And like those children's parents, I find that the ambivalence has become my own.

I anguish over raising my children here; I anguish over other people's children being raised here. Last summer, around the corner from our house a dead man lay in a vacant lot for at least twenty-four hours before anyone realized something must be very wrong. The sight of an intoxicated man sacked out on the ground along the city's main street in Newburgh is too common to elicit immediate reaction. Finally, children at play alerted the police: they had kicked their ball too close too many times for him not to stir. Another impromptu street shrine, littered with candles, balloons, and stuffed animals, soon cluttered the sidewalk.

It becomes easy to understand the motives of families who have left. Tempted to flee this place I too want to escape this pocket of urban misery into the amnesiac comfort of the suburbs or the anonymity of another state. But with each wave of exodus, Newburgh is again impoverished, losing her most valuable wealth: her people.

As I piece together shards of narrative, a twin betrayal beckons. Various splinters of memory that have been embedded and sealed over, with time, resurface. The mind resists their recollection, and again I am tempted to flee, this time into the neighborhood of falsehood. Memory demands to tell its story with nostalgia but without sentimentality, while history asks for complexity devoid of complacency. If, like the mainstream media, I glamorize a ghetto environment, I am untrue to the place of my childhood that more resembled a rural town in the deep South than an inner city. A snapshot of our neighbors drinking sweet iced tea on their ramshackle porch, watching the lazy progress of ships on the river some sultry summer afternoon, might easily have been taken for a portrait from the South. Conversely, if I romanticize the noble poor in this setting of natural beauty, as if both people and environment were unspoiled by contamination, I mislead readers.

Navigating the small raft of my story on the wide bed of the river's waters, I cannot offer a comprehensive history of Newburgh. Rather, I want to sketch a geography of the city that haunts me. Even as I write, the map washes away under my pen like writing in sand. The present seeps into the past, or the past floods the present. Waves of comings and goings crash into each other, episodes of welcome and defeat. In response to my question, "What good can come out of Newburgh?" I have been graced with stories of others in exodus, living and dead. Greedily taking in the ever-changing colors of the river, I am gifted with poetry in exile — the language of the dispossessed.

I have resisted this journey of return, but my mind wandered here anyway, lured by the tides that create their own friction in a river that flows both ways. Brought back to Newburgh, I follow — often unwillingly — because it is here that Christ beckons to me. Whether here or in exodus from here, my heart chokes on raw memory. The past scars as it heals. Limbs once broken must be set properly. I am here to be reshaped as a writer, to reset these broken bones into a lasting fit. I am here because this exile demands a return; this exodus, obedience. Like the disciple who had a hard time believing the Messiah could come out of Nazareth, I wonder where salvation can be encountered in this distressed inner city. I wonder where *my* salvation can be found. In the end, the answer is an invitation: "Come and see."

A Priceless View

Part One

EXILE

** *One* **

Beginnings

Psalm 126 sings,

> *When the Lord restored the fortunes of Zion,*
> *we were like those who dream.*
> *Then our mouth was filled with laughter,*
> *and our tongue with shouts of joy;*
> *then it was said among the nations,*
> *"The Lord has done great things for them."*
> *The Lord has done great things for us,*
> *and we rejoiced.*

The first time I drove alone into Newburgh from the nearby town to which my husband and daughter and I had just moved, I gripped the steering wheel tightly. My pulse was racing as my knuckles turned white at the wheel. Whirring in my head, conflicting thoughts collided into one another. Approaching the east end of the city, where the Spanish-speaking parish we had started attending was located, I drove with extra caution. This section of the city is so small, its main streets so easily accessible, I couldn't get lost, but my heart pounded anyway. My practical fear was to avoid both potholes and pedestrians (who in this neighborhood often walk into the street without looking, in thoughtless bravado or practiced defiance). My inarticulate anxiety was the fear of coming across someone from my childhood. How could I traverse years of estrangement, to explain the obvious: What was I doing here?

Over these several years I have come across many old friends and neighbors from my childhood. Most greetings have been surprised, briefly joyous, then casual — almost anticlimactic after years of imagining this, my return. Only in bits and pieces have I reassembled the current lives of people I once loved. At the end of our first year teaching religious education to teenagers in the parish, my husband, Kenney, and I were leaving the school when we bumped into the mother of one of his students.

Sandy and I stared at one another for a long time before words finally came. In grammar school we had been the best of friends, and now here she was, with two teenage daughters and a young son. Her family had been one of the first of many in the area to come here from Peru. She was just as surprised to hear me speaking fluent Spanish as I was to hear her speaking fluent English! I learned that in the year my family moved away, Sandy became pregnant with her first daughter. She married a young man from one of the first Mexican families to move here, and the birth of their second daughter followed shortly after. Obtaining her GED and working as one of the first bilingual tellers in a local bank, she now works for a law firm. Still living in Newburgh, Sandy has put down roots here in a way that I, long absent, have not. She and her children represent the city's future while I remain bound to its past.

I BEGAN TO THINK that if I could just decode the city's history, prying open its closed chapters, I could find some clues that would make my life here — past and present — intelligible. Forcing myself to study its past, in all its forgotten glories and ongoing contradictions, I tried to force the city too to reveal itself. Was I searching for evidence of its worthiness, in order to explain my love for a city that does not merit my loyalty? Or, knowing this stay might be temporary, was I looking for proof that Newburgh deserves its relentless fate of being abandoned by successive generations? Either way, my intuition told me that if I did not dive into its archives (and into my own stored memories), I would never be free. Newburgh would continue to haunt me.

MY EXPLORATION BEGAN with a glimpse into prehistory. Twenty thousand years ago, the entire region of the Northeast lay buried under the Wisconsin ice sheet. As ice dissipated during the next few thousand years, Long Island Sound and the Lower Hudson River were exposed as freshwater lakes. The weight of the ice sheet — which by now had retreated north to Albany — pressed on the terrain, allowing water from the Great Lakes and the Champlain Lowland to flow into the Hudson River Valley. Until about six or seven thousand years ago, when the melting of the glaciers slowed, the ocean regularly rose to inundate this part of the valley.

Fresh water, flowing southward, was met by salt water from the Atlantic Ocean. Here at this precise juncture of the river valley, salt and fresh water still mingle: surface waters flow seaward over the salt water that travels inward from the ocean. This river ecosystem, which once teemed abundantly with whales, porpoises, shellfish, and even seals, is the promised land of an ancient legend: in the rendering of a Native American myth of origin, a group of nomads was told to wander until they found "the river that runs both ways."

Prehistory careens into history when European explorers, their annals recording the "discovery" of the New World, arrived to the Hudson River Valley. In search of a northwest passage to the Pacific, in 1609, Henry Hudson scanned the landscape at just this particular bend in the Hudson River. He stood with his sailors on the ship's deck, taking in the bounty of river and land. The abundance of trees alone must have astonished them: a dozen varieties of oaks and four of hickory; pines, firs, and evergreens; sassafras, mountain laurel, red pine, sycamore, white elm, magnolia, dogwood, mulberry, maple, river birch, walnut, and witch hazel. The landscape's rolling skirt unfurled at the edge of waters teeming with any fisherman's dream catch: plentiful oysters, cobalt-jointed blue crabs, majestic leaping sturgeons, darting shad, and a countless variety of middle-size fish.

From the ship's deck, Hudson and his crew surveyed the rising mountains on either shore. Looking in the direction of what would later become Newburgh, he remarked that this would be "a pleasant place to build a town upon."

I HAVE OFTEN WONDERED if the land formation of the Bluff existed then, so many hundreds of years ago. It is visible to the eye from the river, and surely he would have seen it from the deck of his ship. Here history gives way to my own memories. The recent past intrudes upon the colonial past. The "pleasant place" Hudson might have been eyeing — a huge, flat ledge of grass at the top of a cliff extending upward from the river's edge along the western bank — may be the same site of my recurring dreams.

As my brother and I would approach our neighborhood as we walked home from grammar school, the mountains rose taller before our eyes with each step. Though the river was still hidden out of view until the last block, we could already catch sight of the Bluff, the large expanse of grass across the street from our house. Drawing nearer, we would glimpse a ribbon of water that grew wider as we came closer. Depending on the day, the river might appear blue, green, gray, silver, or even brown; it might shimmer with the mischievous, sharp edges of waves catching sunlight or it might glow with a flat, tranquil veneer plated across its surface. Sometimes fog covered the mountains, at times hanging in a heavy curtain of cloud. Other times the mist drifted sheer and fine, a bridal veil sweeping across the mountain's velvet green shoulders. The looming mountains meant we had almost arrived to the safety of our neighborhood. The widening band of river meant we were close to home.

From here, just about to turn the bend to arrive at our own block, the trouble spots had all been passed — yards where vicious dogs, snarling, strained at their leashes, a house where two belligerent sisters sneered at passersby, the corner store where older boys known to be troublemakers gathered. Relief lightened our steps. A hello might be called out from an adult gardening outside or a child already home from school. If it were the warmer half of the year, coming to our street we would be greeted by the sight and smell of Dolly's roses.

Since our neighbor Dolly and her husband owned the corner plot, and because their house sat to the far right side of the property, they owned a sizeable patch of green space bordering the sidewalk on two sides of the block. Here they cultivated several fragrant varieties of roses in shades of red, yellow, and pink. The blooms blossomed long before and past the usual growing season, tended by Dolly's faithful husband, Garrett. My mother often asked their secret. Pesticides and artificial fertilizers alone could not explain their success. Everyone agreed, Garrett had a way with roses. Walking along the sidewalk regaled by their fragrance, we turned the corner and came home.

Psalm 126 concludes,

> *Restore our fortunes, O Lord,*
> *like the watercourses in the Negeb.*
> *May those who sow in tears*
> *reap with shouts of joy.*
> *Those who go out weeping,*
> *bearing the seed for sowing,*
> *shall come home with shouts of joy,*
> *carrying their sheaves.*

MY PARENTS HAD MOVED HERE from New York City because they hoped Newburgh would be an ideal place to raise a family. They had been looking for a place to settle within commuting distance of my father's job. As a small city with a population comparable to that of just one neighborhood in Manhattan or Brooklyn (around thirty-five thousand inhabitants), Newburgh looked like an attractive alternative. With its scenic panorama for grown-ups to enjoy and its outdoor places for kids to explore, it might prove liveable, my parents thought, for a family with young children. There were few houses that they could afford, but that didn't matter — only one was needed, and they had fallen in love with this one.

Built in the style of a Queen Anne modified Victorian, the house's first-floor facade was made of stone and the upper stories of brick. The heaviness of its wraparound stone front porch with wood floor (an inviting place for neighborhood kids to play) was relieved by slender Romanesque columns painted white, while stained-glass detail sparkled just above the front door. Not readily visible, but seen immediately once one entered the house, a larger stained-glass piece in the shape of an arc glimmered above the stairway leading to the second floor. Two garrets rose above the roof, as well as the chimney from the dining room fireplace.

The most arresting feature of the house, however, was three huge panels of bay windows that looked out onto the river and the mountains from the master bedroom on the second story. My parents, whose bedroom it was, prized the panorama that was my mother's daily delight and the envy of her city-dwelling friends. Coming home from one of his many trips, my father would stand in the center of the triad of windows and take a long look at the river and mountains he had left, to which he had returned.

The house had once belonged to the administrator of a local business school of some reputation. Proponents of the Spencer School boasted that its alumni never needed to look for work: *they* were sought by prospective employers. "Old Man Turner" lived here until his death, at which time the house passed hands. Subsequent owners inflicted various indignities on our poor house (such as laying wall-to-wall carpeting over parquet floors), which my mother took to heart as if she had been present to witness them. In hearing her recount these atrocities, one felt convinced that they were, indeed, inexcusable. To her, the house represented a gem to be mined and polished, or — better still — a hostage to be rescued from insufferable, almost perverse bad taste.

Coming home from school we might find her stripping paint off the woodwork of the stair banister or hammering some miscreant molding into place. One day we came home to find my mother ripping up the linoleum in the living room. She had suspected that wood floors lay underneath this ochre-and-yellow-patterned flooring, but the exquisite parquet design she glimpsed underneath surpassed expectation. Triumphantly tearing wide swatches apart with her strong hands and dumping them in the garbage, she urged us onto our hands and knees to join her. After months of scraping off the gook that had held the linoleum in place, then sanding the floor by hand, and finally, laying down a glaze, the honey-colored wood floor edged by a contrasting brown ribbon pattern was restored to its former glory.

My mother too grew roses; the patches of earth just outside our huge gray front porch held just enough space for three rosebushes on either side of the stone steps. While they did not smell as fragrant as Dolly's, nor bloom as luxuriously, she coaxed them along during the growing season and protected them with burlap coverings in the winter.

Neighbors

Our section of the city, called the Washington Heights (in shorter form, simply "the Heights") for the headquarters where George and Martha Washington had once spent a year and a half, had been built backwards: this strip of houses, the farthest from the downtown, had been among the first constructed. Mansions along the Bluff with its magnificent view of the river once housed prosperous families and their servants. As industry thrived and more and more workers' homes were needed, additional houses filled in the space between the Bluff and the downtown area of the city.

By the year my parents moved to Newburgh, many factories had already moved out, and these neighborhoods already showed signs of decline. Some houses were bought at inexpensive prices by incoming families from other countries or from the South, while others were bought by landlords and used as rental property. Though similar to the rest of the city in being racially diverse, our neighborhood was different in that we had a higher rate of owner occupancy. At the time my family lived in the Heights, all five houses on our block were owner-occupied.

To the left, four generations of an African-American family who had come from North Carolina long before my own family moved to Newburgh lived in Dolly's wooden A-frame painted gray with green trim. Two little girls, Janice and Letisha, often stayed there with their grandmother in the attic apartment. Their great-aunts and great-great-aunts escaped the summer heat by coming downstairs to sit on the porch.

To the right, a duplex with a large front porch and stone facade housed two elderly white women. One, of slight build and affectionate nature, rented her side of the house from the other. The other woman, handsomely aristocratic with waist-length snow-white hair that she wore in one long winding coil, presided over the neighborhood association. Her middle-aged retarded son, dubbed Mayor Mickey, supervised the block. (To our chagrin, my mother once in a while asked him to baby-sit me and my brother.) Mayor Mickey took his responsibility for the Heights quite seriously. If he noticed that a neighbor's lawn mower had been running off kilter, unbidden he would take it apart, make a diagnosis, and then inform its owner how the dismantled machinery should be fixed.

On the other corner plot a gray Cape Cod style house was home to another elderly white neighbor, a Quaker, whose grown children had long moved out of the area. Imagining how it would spruce up the neighborhood and thinking she would be pleasantly surprised by his initiative, Mayor Mickey determined to do this neighbor a "favor." He arranged for a contractor to repair her driveway while she was gone for a week. He couldn't understand why she was so angry upon returning to a freshly repaved driveway — for which she had to pay the bill!

Among these elderly neighbors, chances were that in clement weather someone would be seated on their front porch. Most afternoons, each house would have a lawn chair or rocker set out. From here the neighborhood elders took in the view of the river, commenting to each other about its changes in color and movement. Quick to protect lawns and yards from overly rambunctious children or pets, they also clucked at an occasional car speeding by or remonstrated playmates who were not getting along properly. (If we were to play with any privacy, we had to escape to the woods over the Bluff.) The grown-ups corrected us children sparingly but freely, and we learned to take correction from adults other than our parents. Color differences made no distinction in this unwritten rule. Any child who disrespected an elder would catch severe trouble at home.

Once my mother had restored the two back apartments sufficiently to make them habitable, we had tenants whose rent helped toward our mortgage payments. At one point a couple with a young daughter moved in. I loved them both, the woman for introducing me to e.e. cummings and the Harlem Renaissance Poets and the man for his dream of claiming the oldest church building in the city, the Dutch Reformed church (a national historical landmark), as a cultural center.

The small knot of girls with whom I mostly played lived nearby, its porous boundaries allowing for ongoing reconfiguration as friends came and went. The two little girls who lived next door were joined by two sisters in subsequent years. Sometimes their mother kept them with her during the week, and Janice and Letisha came to spend weekends in the attic apartment with their grandmother; other years, they lived with her during the week and went back to their mother on Fridays. Their cousin, Luanne, belonged to *three* houses: her mother's house across town, overcrowded with her many brothers and sisters of whom she numbered among the youngest; the house of the aunt who raised her as a child, just down the street along the Bluff; and Dolly's house, where she was put to work caring for their elderly relatives who could not feed, dress, or bathe themselves. Members of their large extended family often came to visit, so there were usually other cousins around as well.

Just around the corner, in the house bordering Dolly's roses, my friend Ruby (a dark-skinned girl as exquisite as her name) and her half-sister, Nicole, lived with their parents and their younger brother. Although this family did not have a lot of relatives in Newburgh, they took in a succession of foster children, and so there were often other kids from their household, too. A more temporary addition to our group came when a family with a girl about my age moved from Puerto Rico into an apartment across the street from them. The new family stayed only about a year before going back, discouraged by their efforts to start a new life here. When Ruby and Nicole's mother visited to welcome them to the neighborhood, she found the family living in an unfurnished apartment, sleeping on bare floors. She organized a collection of mattresses, kitchen items, and other household furnishings, to which all the families around were asked to contribute.

A friend from school, Angelique, who looked after her three little siblings while her grandmother worked a factory job, sometimes joined us from up the block. She and I had a special bond because we were among the few kids from our neighborhood to attend Catholic school. Another friend of ours, Marisol, was sometimes allowed to come over from a couple of streets away, though she was never allowed to stay until evening.

As an adult looking back, I can understand now in a way that I could not then why Angelique's grandmother and Marisol's parents did not give them even the limited freedom I enjoyed. In Angelique's case, since she and her very young brother and two sisters were being raised by her grandmother, and since her grandmother had to work to support the household, free time was a luxury they couldn't afford. In Marisol's case, her parents (recently arrived from Puerto Rico) thought that allowing her to enter the fray of the neighborhood would bring her into contact with all the urban problems they feared. In time I would see that they were right.

Elders

> The righteous flourish like the palm tree,
>   and grow like a cedar in Lebanon.
> They are planted in the house of the Lord;
>   they flourish in the courts of our God.
> In old age they still produce fruit;
>   they are always green and full of sap,
> showing that the Lord is upright;
>   God is my rock, in whom there is no unrighteousness.
> — Psalm 92

In the summers, we girls used to pick wildflowers to give to our elderly neighbors, whom we called "the ladies," which would sometimes merit an invitation to come inside. Fascinated by the fading black and white pictures of young women with vaguely familiar faces in bridal gowns, we gingerly sat at the edge of our seats in dusty parlors or squirmed at the uncomfortable intimacy of a kitchen table, trying not to spill cookie crumbs.

The ladies' homes were filled with fascinating objects: displayed sets of dishes, furniture with doilies draped on arms and backs, old-fashioned utensils in carefully orchestrated kitchens. Luanne's great-great-aunt, Aunt Nellie, lived on the floor below Janice and Letisha's grandmother's attic. In her living room, elephant statues stood in the place of end tables, and velvet paintings of African scenes hung where our white neighbors might have placed bland oil-on-canvas landscapes, but the atmosphere of each elderly lady's home was recognizable all the same: sacred domestic space. Always there were crocheted afghans, pillows of novel sizes and fabrics, coasters for drinks (one would never dream of committing the heinous crime of setting a cup directly on a table and lace curtains at the windows.

The most daunting aspect of these visits for us children was that they required not only good manners, but the wearing of shoes, to which we had grown unaccustomed by the time wildflowers were in bloom. As soon as the weather became warm enough for us to play outside, most of us girls went barefoot. Upon coming home we would take off our school shoes, which — as our mothers often reminded us — had to last as long as possible. With the exception of Ruby (who managed to do everything gracefully), we awkwardly kicked off flimsy plastic shoes like jellies or flip-flops from the discount store in order to better run, jump double Dutch, or slide down the woods of the Bluff. By the time the end of the school year arrived, my feet would be calloused enough to go bare all day long, even resisting the scorching pavement. Soles blackened with tar and dirt, I would have to scrub them before putting on the shoes, which felt foreign and stiff and that added to the discomfort and formality of visits to "the ladies."

If our neighborhood exhibited a distinctly matriarchal character, with the presence of several elderly women and mothers and grandmothers visibly taking charge of the environment which governed us, it also reflected an absence of fathers. Of course, the three elderly ladies in the houses to the right had been widowed, and so had many of the elderly women who shared close quarters in Dolly's house to the left of us. My brother's friends' father was a truck driver, and so spent much time on the road; other neighborhood dads kept busy with side jobs, apart from their full-time jobs, to make ends meet. My own father commuted an hour away and frequently made trips, even internationally, for his work. But it did not take much to figure out that many of the worst-off families (who lived in rented apartments where, as Ruby and Nicole's mother said, "The landlord should pay *them* to live there") depended on a single parent. In every case we knew of, this parent was a mother. The lucky kids among them also had a grandmother who could be counted on to help raise them. (This trend has only intensified in the years since I grew up in Newburgh. In 1990, fully a third of all families was estimated to be headed by a single caretaker. Currently, almost half of the students in the school district, 5,600 kids out of 12,200, are poor enough to enroll in the public schools' free lunch program.)

While my parents found a source of scandal in the fact that Janice and Letisha and, in later years their two sisters, were born of different fathers, some of the other neighborhood women viewed their free-spirited mother more indulgently. "She's too young to be tied down with all those kids," they allowed, adding how fortunate it was that the girls' grandmother had company in her old age. Such memories reflect not only the strong personalities of working-class women of diverse backgrounds but also the resigned determination of mothers who know that the family's being held together — and any chance of the children's growing up into functional adults — rested on their shoulders.

The women in the neighborhood viewed two suspected cases of domestic violence much more seriously. On different occasions they dropped hints to the two wives as if to encourage them to seek help, but to no avail. Among themselves, the neighborhood women commiserated openly about the injustice of this abuse. They hooted with laughter about how once when Janice and Letisha's mother's boyfriend came after her in a fit of anger, lunging up the stairs toward the attic apartment, their grandmother had dashed a pot of scalding water on him.

Although it seemed that not much could be done for the women in our neighborhood who stayed in abusive relationships, awareness of the problem served as catalyst for opening the first shelter for abused women in the city. A local woman who herself suffered from cerebral palsy — a condition that instead of debilitating her only seemed to fuel her compassion for others — championed the efforts. Ruby's parents donated a building, and many of us kids were pressed into service. I remember scraping, painting, and cleaning to make the home habitable. Before we were put to work for the day, we had to pray the rosary (the organizers of the project, including Ruby's mother, belonged to the Legion of Mary) amid cardboard boxes, tarps, and tools in the mess that would be transformed slowly before our eyes into a living room.

I also remember being seated at Dolly's table for a different type of indoctrination. Once we neighborhood girls reached a certain age, she wanted to make sure we understood our dignity as women. Like a merchant convinced of the value of her wares, she drilled us on what women must do to assert themselves. She made us repeat after her, "What's his is mine, but what's mine is mine." Dolly gave us a concrete example: she had found out through gossip that her husband, Garrett, had been seen driving around town with another woman. Imparting sternly that she did not care if he had an affair, she threatened to kick him out if he used "her" car to do it.

WE SPENT SLOW, HOT summer mornings inside to avoid the heat of the sun, then long, lazy afternoons on someone's porch, sucking ice or braiding one another's hair. As the afternoon cooled, the games would begin in earnest. Our favorites were double

Dutch, dodgeball, and "hot mama" (played by choosing a person who would chase her "children" with a switch, crying out "hot mama" as warning). My brother and his friends took over the Bluff for Frisbee games when they weren't scrambling in the woods or fishing in the creek.

The tempo of the play picked up as the day's heat wound down. We were joined on summer nights by clusters of other kids from around the neighborhood. There was one group from down the street, who lived in houses farther along the Bluff, and another group — this one comprised of rougher kids — from around the corner up the street. During my earlier years, we trapped fireflies ("lightning bugs") in jars or played catch-as-catch-can, which started with one person as "it," tagging others, who in turn tagged others, and ended when the last person who had not yet been tagged declared victory. As we grew older, playing cards became our favorite pastime, with Spades and Hearts championships on our stone front porch lasting far into the night until someone's mother finally chased everyone off to bed.

Real Estate

> *I was glad when they said to me,*
> *"Let us go to the house of the Lord!"*
> *Our feet are standing*
> *within your gates, O Jerusalem.*

I gathered these fragments of the past in my heart on a visit back to the street where we had run over the scorching pavement with bare feet so many summer nights. My husband accompanied me, eager to see for himself the home I had so often described. When Kenney, who often drives around Newburgh for his work, told me about the "For Sale" sign displayed on the overgrown front lawn, I had called the real estate company. Not letting on that my family had once lived there, I made an appointment for us to see the house (now priced at literally ten times the amount my parents paid for it years ago). The surreptitious viewing gave us the motive for a visit back to my old neighborhood.

As we drove I took in the state of the neighborhood, the sinking feeling in my stomach growing stronger block by block. More houses had been abandoned, their windows boarded over and walls spray painted with graffiti. On a positive note, more cars line the sidewalks than when I was a child.

We approached the familiar block as my brother and I used to (but I was behind the wheel this time), and the mountains once again rose, broad-shouldered, before me. It was from just the same distance from which I would first sight the river's wide expanse of water when coming home from school. I couldn't help noticing how the water widened much more quickly from a car window than from a pedestrian's vantage. My husband drew in his breath sharply. Here it was — right in front of us! — the most spectacular bend in the Hudson Valley in all its majesty.

My eyes, however, took in changes measured against the store of memory. While the river commanded attention as magnificently as ever, the Bluff had fared poorly. Perhaps because it was still winter, the color of the grass had a listless quality to it, while the berry bushes and honeysuckle jungle that used to burst into abundance each spring were nowhere to be seen. And perhaps because these are, after all, childhood memories, the wide-open area of grass along the cliff seemed much smaller than I remembered. But even after taking these realizations into account, I had to admit that the Bluff that had awakened my sense of freedom had deteriorated. The soil of the woods at the meadow's edge had eroded, lengthening the slope down to the river's edge and shortening the meadow considerably. The house on the corner that had belonged to one of my favorite "ladies," the Quaker, once so primly maintained with fresh paint, now looked worn and tired, its gray coat peeling. Its driveway repaved as a coming-home surprise needed patching. I knew that the house had been sold once she could no longer live there on her own, but the shock of its disrepair startled me. Similarly, I knew that both Dolly and Garrett had died years ago but was unprepared for the mournful sight of the few crippled rosebushes that had survived their deaths. The brave grandmother of the two little girls had died. Aunt Nellie too had died. I wondered vaguely what had happened to the elephant statues. Dolly's house stood with windows boarded up and plywood nailed over the screened-in porch.

We had heard years ago that the aristocratic woman with her coil of snowy white hair had died. Her son, Mayor Mickey, who stayed on to continue supervising the block, was the sole neighbor left from my family's time. That whole generation of elders, vigilant in rocking chairs on front porches, bent on civilizing us for posterity's sake, was gone. There would be no more fragrant blooms to welcome me to this block. Lastly, I faced the house with the great stone porch. Yard disheveled, perennials uncared for, the home of my childhood stood forlorn. The only remaining evidence of my mother's own rosebushes consisted of withered stumps barely discernible in a patch of overgrown weeds.

The real estate agent pulled up in a metallic gold-colored car. He quickly sized us up, assuming (probably for the simple fact that we are white) that we were interested in the house as rental property. Without pausing to take in the breathtaking view of the river and the mountains, he glanced, rather, at his watch: he was late. Locking his car doors and casting apprehensive glances up and down the street, he clucked in disgust over the litter in the gutter. He led us up the great stone steps, and we followed, docile. Heart pounding, I ascended the stairs and found myself on the front porch of my childhood for the first time since we had moved away. The agent fumbled with a fistful of keys that jingled in his hands. As he unlocked the front door (painted an unthinkable red) with its familiar lion-head knocker, we went inside.

I had seen pictures of the house's restoration, begun by my mother but continued by the man who had bought the house from my parents — an interior decorator by profession — so I was not as shocked as I might have been by the changes. The hallway with its stained-glass window shaped like an arc and the wooden banister leading upstairs looked the same, but the living room area had been changed. Knocking out the wall between the hallway and the dining room, the interior decorator had created one large, open space separated only by the wall of the fireplace. Wall-to-wall mirrors enhanced the impression of spaciousness and light. The subsequent owner had also remodeled the lavatory, refurbishing the tiny room in an understated art deco style that surprisingly suited the space quite well. In the dining area, he had put a border of flowered wallpaper along its walls, and the design he had chosen and the delicacy with which it had been placed so matched the spirit of this old Queen Anne style modified Victorian that I realized suddenly that he too had understood this house. But that had been before the house was sold yet again, this time as rental property.

The Census of the Year 2000 calculated that 58 percent of the population in Newburgh pays rent, but in the poorest neighborhoods, like the Washington Heights, the figure measures up to 68 percent. Of 10,476 housing units, only about 2,800 are owner-occupied. There are 1,332 vacant housing units in Newburgh in boarded-up buildings that not even a slumlord dares to exploit.

With a pang, I surveyed the flooring: the parquet that my mother had so painstakingly restored had been covered over once again, this time with cheap, slate-colored linoleum. The magnificent fireplace had been boarded over with planks, its walnut mantelpiece scarred. Ironically, the openness of the space and the effect of the mirroring served to intensify the sense of clutter strewn about. The living room was obviously being used as a bedroom for a family, from the evidence of clothes, stuffed animals, and sheets and blankets on the couch. The kitchen appliances looked old and crusted over. I wondered if they were the same old ones my family had put in.

The second floor looked even worse. The fireplace in the master bedroom was covered over, no longer operative. My bedroom was locked with a padlock, from which I surmised that yet another renter had made my old room a home within a home. We trudged upstairs to the third floor. The attic rooms, hot and stuffy as ever, held more clothes and beds. It seemed that several people lived up there, too. After casting a hasty glance over the disorder, we descended. The stairs to the attic had always been creaky but now were made treacherous by several missing planks. The final travesty awaited us where we ended the tour, at the huge bay windows overlooking the Bluff: one of the panes was cracked and had been covered over with cardboard and masking tape.

As we stood there, the real estate agent, perhaps noticing my dismay at the state of the house and mistaking it for commercial concern, insinuated how many rents could be collected from this house. Why, its current owners were renting the attic as a separate apartment (even though it had neither a bathroom nor cooking facilities). Adding the studio and the upstairs apartment in the back, that made four rental units. He deftly calculated how many months it would take for the rent alone to pay for the buying price of the house. As I stood, dazed, looking out the bay windows on the unchanging panorama of my childhood, Kenney pressed my arm in silent sympathy.

The real estate agent finally fell quiet and, for the first time since we had arrived, glanced outside, too. The three of us watched the mid-afternoon light of winter play on the water, the silver edges of waves flashing as the clouds parted briefly over the brown shoulders of barren mountains. After a moment he concluded the sales pitch: "The house isn't in such great shape, and face it, the neighborhood sucks. But just look at that million-dollar view." How could those few words fall so flat and yet ring so true? I wondered. Silently, I corrected him: It's not a million-dollar view. It's priceless.

Awakenings

> Lord, you have been our dwelling place
>> in all generations.
> Before the mountains were brought forth,
>> or ever you had formed the earth and the world,
>> from everlasting to everlasting you are God.

38

You turn us back to dust,
and say, "Turn back, you mortals."
For a thousand years in your sight
are like yesterday when it is past,
or like a watch in the night.
— Psalm 90

As I later remembered contemplating the beloved view of the
Hudson River outside what had once been my parents' bedroom
window, I was amazed to find it so perfectly recognizable. Every
undulation of Mt. Beacon's range and the exact proportion of
land to sky had been engraved permanently into my memory in
the relatively short years of my childhood. Each shadow, each swell
of earth on the mountains seemed to speak to me of comfort and
familiarity. As if a sigh held for many years were being released,
my breath exhaled in silent thanksgiving for the beauty before us.
In a lucid moment, I thought to wonder at its longevity. Just how
everlasting are these everlasting hills and river? As I studied the
valley's evolution, the answers astounded me.

The ice sheet that once covered this region began to dissipate
twenty thousand years ago, but the life of the Hudson River may
extend back an inconceivable 240 million years. Geologists dis-
agree as to whether the river has always flowed the same course,
but it is thought that the Hudson River Highlands, among which
Newburgh is nestled, were once buried under a shallow sea reaching to Mexico. Mount Beacon and Storm King face each other
from opposite banks across the river's waters, but they are both
formed by the same ancient granitic gneiss. The "million-dollar
view" is millions of years old. The process of evolution that created
it is priceless.

OUR BIOREGION, rich in woods, marsh, creeks, mountain, and
fields gave us kids a natural habitat so lush that we could easily
forget we lived in an inner city. Dolly gave us one kind of indoctrination, and the nuns at our Catholic grammar another, but
the environment too educated us. Our natural environs, although

altered by generations of human necessity, greed, and invention, still preserved an integrity compelling in its own right. The margins where human and natural progress met made the most exciting places to play: the creeks, railroad tunnels, and woods at the edge of the Bluff. Luring us to try out the limits of wildness, it called us to taste freedom and danger.

The boys were excused from Dolly's conversations, which is just as well, since at that age they could hardly be restrained to stay indoors, and when home, they tended "pets" they had brought home — crayfish, turtles, snakes, or frogs. Every day they explored the woods of the Bluff, roaming its trails down to the busy road and the railroad tracks parallel to the river banks. Running at breakneck speed, they hurtled themselves down the cliff's side, having calculated exactly (through bruising trial-and-error) which trees could be counted on to brace them at the last moment before they crashed into a dense patch of woods. My brother and his friends took the game a step farther, and jumped, crying "Geronimo!" into thickets that housed the honeysuckle, blackcaps, and other berries that we girls used to make pretend perfumes and jams.

To the far right off the Bluff, we could sight Bannerman's Island, a small island to the south made fascinating by its castle in ruins. Its owner, an eccentric industrialist, stored a collection of antique weapons in his home, which he had designed to resemble a Scottish castle. He had also amassed a fair amount of dynamite, which exploded one warm day when a fire somehow started. By some miracle there were no casualties: Mr. Bannerman was gone for the day, and Mrs. Bannerman, sunning herself on the far end of the island, narrowly escaped death when she rose from her hammock — crushed moments later by a flying parapet — to go for an iced tea. My brother and his friends speculated about how much dynamite must have been stored, what the Bannermans had planned to do with it, and what other types of arms had been stockpiled. We girls daydreamed more romantically about what a castle might look like, with furnishings, gardens, and perhaps even a fountain.

Another pastime that the boys, especially, enjoyed was trespassing onto the property of factories along the river banks. They loved to scout the environs of plants that dumped leftovers into the woods or the creek: a felt factory, a battery plant, a wax factory that specialized in voodoo candles. Salvaging votives shaped like roosters or skulls in black or cobalt blue, they melted down the wax under my mother's careful eye and poured it into molds made from discarded beer cans.

Sometimes we girls joined them on these adventures. We often tagged along on trips to the railroad tracks. Placing pennies and nickels (garnered from our parents' spare change) on the silver tracks, we lay in wait for the train cars that would charge past and squash them. Once flattened, we snatched them, piping hot, from the silver tracks to examine the smooth, oblong surfaces burning into the palms of our hands.

An enormous dark tunnel, like the huge wing of a black bird, sat forebodingly — irresistibly — across the road. We often entered its mysterious cool interior. Eyes momentarily blinded, we needed a while to become adjusted to sudden nightfall. The dank spray of the river, so close, blended with the sooty odor of train tracks and the sharp, fecund smell of overgrown vegetation. There was always the chance that a train would come before we had walked the entire length of the tunnel, in which case we had to plaster our bodies against the walls, hearts thumping, while the engine and its cars whooshed past our rib cages flattened against cool black bricks. Our palms and backs would be black with soot, but the exhilarating rush of the trains left our throats excitingly dry and heads pleasantly giddy. No matter how stern the injunction from those parents wise enough to discern how their children had gotten elbows and pant seats so filthy, nothing could deter us from the pull of that tunnel.

I once accompanied my brother on a fishing excursion to the creek down the Bluff on a day his friends were otherwise occupied. (After all, I was two and a half years younger and, unforgivably, a girl.) Sorting through his elaborate gear, he selected a mess of flyers, rods, reels, wires, and hooks from a singularly fishy-smelling tackle box made of green plastic. I was put in charge of a tangled fistful of golden fishing line, which I stashed in a pocket and fingered as we went along. Loaded with equipment, which in spite of our best efforts kept getting tangled, we scrambled down the trail into the woods until we reached the creek.

Since it was spring, when the water level was highest, the creek was gushing. The rocks at the bottom of the creek bed were uneven and slippery, making it tricky to keep one's balance. Wading across, I lost my footing and grabbed at my brother. We both went into the cold, rank water. He quickly grabbed me above the elbow and yanked me up to the surface. Except for the patient, gloating way my brother showed me how to pierce earthworms onto rusty hooks, I remember little else from that day but those few brief seconds of drifting helplessly, carried by a current that I could not fight, with a terrifying nothingness under my unanchored feet. When I recovered, I groped for the golden line in my pocket — and found it still there.

That day we ran across men doing "real" fishing. Their catch might have included a mummichog (found from the Gulf of St. Lawrence to Texas, but which never strays more than a few hundred feet from where it hatched) or a sole (known to travel from Massachusetts all the way to the eastern shores of Panama). These men, who themselves had come from somewhere else, depended on the day's catch to feed their families — even though local residents had been warned not to consume fish from the polluted river. From an early age, then, I learned that beauty and exploitation surged in the same waters. I learned too that immersion was inevitable. As we emerged from the creek, our damp clothes and hair emitted the creek's rank odor. But the treasure, a thread fingered surreptitiously in my pocket, remained. The single, brilliant strand, even if it was hopelessly tangled, would not save me from the current but represented, somehow, a brilliant, inner resourcefulness that had to be preserved at all costs.

THE CREEK'S WATERS smelled rank not only because of natural decomposition, which makes river areas fertile, but because of sewage released into its streams. Its rocks were slimy due not only to algae, but also to the chemical wastes dumped by factories on its banks. During my family's time in Newburgh, the environmental crisis of the Hudson River hit a peak of public awareness. Although I was too young to remember it, there had been a drought for four years and the water table was so low that human and industrial wastes reeked. Suddenly, residents of the Hudson Valley started to realize that many forms of life depended on the river's well-being.

Industrial polluting of the river had gone on for decades already before my childhood. Government leaders seemed afraid to challenge offending companies, especially since many businesses were already leaving New York in search of cheaper labor. From the 1950s to the late 1970s, several tons of the poisonous metal cadmium were dumped into a river cove. One environmentalist growing up across the river in the 1950s remembered the creek leading to the river changing color every day — depending on the dye being dumped by the local fabric plant. Kepone, a highly toxic insecticide, ran off from agricultural areas into the waters, and DDT was discovered in the river in 1970. My brother remembers our teachers in school teaching us to mouth the unfamiliar acronym "DDT."

The campaign to clean up the Hudson River was launched by a singular ship whose sails floated across the river of my childhood. When the folk singer Pete Seeger spoke on a late-night television show of his dream to clean up the Hudson River, the show's host laughed out loud. Incredulous, guests from the audience listened to Seeger's strategy. His goal was to clean up the Hudson by encouraging people to sail on its waters. If they spent time with the river, he reasoned, not only would the river get cleaned up: surely valley residents would forge a commitment based on a relationship that would *keep* it clean.

The folk singer and others who joined him set out to raise $140,000 to build a replica of a Dutch sloop such as the kind Henry Hudson had sailed when he entered the Hudson River from the wide mouth of the Atlantic. Schoolchildren, local businesses, and community groups all over the valley chipped in. I remember being caught scrounging around my parents' dresser for change to contribute; luckily, my mother forgave this petty theft as she too took a special interest in the campaign. When a fundraiser featuring Pete Seeger was held in the old Dutch Reformed church (the majestic, crumbling building our tenant hoped to convert into a cultural center), my thrifty mother sprang for tickets. Thereafter, whenever we kids on the Bluff saw the full white sails of the *Clearwater*, we would wave to *our* sloop, our champion in the fight to clean up the Hudson.

** *Two* **

Founders

I must have been seven or eight years old, I suppose, when an unforgettable guest came to our house. It was a winter evening, one of those nights the rest of the house was so cold we sat around the fireplace until it was time for bed. My brother, mother, and I sat close to the fire while my father and the guest he had brought home from work remained seated at the dining room round table.

He must have been in his twenties or early thirties. I remember him as a young man, shy, with a hesitant face and uncertain English. At supper we had watched him eat slowly, head and shoulders bent over his food. He would glance up once in a while, eyes running quickly over our faces and then across the room. After the dishes had been cleared, washed, and put away, my mother, brother, and I pulled our chairs up to the fire's warmth, and the young man and my father stayed back in the shadows, talking in low, hushed voices at the big round table. They sat inclined toward each other but not looking up, not looking into each other's faces; they sat with bodies straining toward each other, faces and eyes fixed on their hands folded on top of the table. At first my father would murmur something, voice lifting slightly at the end of his question. The young man would answer steadily, evenly, his body in an attitude of intense concentration. Then after a while the young man began to talk on his own, in one drone of a monologue, twitching his hands at first and then making gestures with them. Head still bent, he would glance at my father as he talked. Suddenly I saw the scars on his face and hands that I had not taken in over dinner. And then I noticed my father's face in the firelight, tears escaping his almost-closed eyes, traveling down his cheeks and onto his own hands, plain with a single shining band on his left hand.

The next morning the young man was gone. I never saw him again. Now I seem to remember he was from Chile, although I'm not certain, because after my mother's explaining something to me in one of her quietest voices, we never spoke of him again.

THROUGHOUT THOSE YEARS, my parents used to take us on visits to see Dorothy Day. They had met, literally, over a soup pot at the Catholic Worker; their love came into being in the shelters, clothing rooms, and soup kitchens of New York City's Lower East Side. Once in a while, on days they knew she would be home at the hospitality house, we would drive down to see the woman who had founded the Catholic Worker.

Unused to long car rides, my brother and I would fidget on the trip, awed by the sheer enormity of "The City" in contrast to Newburgh's small size and population. Once we arrived, my father would scour the streets for a good parking space and we made our way past alcoholics splayed on the Bowery's streets: men lying on sidewalks or huddled in doorways, their clothes and faces grimy. You were supposed to understand these things as you got older.

My mother had usually prepared an offering: a bunch of bananas, maybe, or a soft, full skirt made of heavy cloth in a deep, rich color. While my parents visited endlessly with the many grown-ups, absorbed in movement talk or gossip, my brother and I stood around, bored and uncomfortable in these unfamiliar adult surroundings. We much preferred visits to the cottage Dorothy kept on Staten Island. There, while the grown-ups talked (also, seemingly incessantly), my brother and I collected shells on the beach, wandering on the gray, grainy sand as wind salted with ocean water whipped our clothes and chilled us to the bone.

My father had worked closely with Dorothy since the late 1950s, serving as her secretary and travel companion; at one time, she appointed him editor of the Catholic Worker newspaper. During college, his job as an orderly in a hospital during the night shift gave him plenty of study time. Somehow he came across Dorothy's autobiography, *The Long Loneliness* — a book that struck him like lightning. Dropping everything, he left college and went to see her. She advised him to finish his studies before returning, because, she explained, "You'll be more useful to us that way."

My mother arrived at the community in New York City after a childhood of reading the movement's newspaper, the *Catholic Worker*. My parents courted under Dorothy's watchful eye. She probably felt particularly responsible since she knew my mother's parents, who had helped her start a hospitality house in Cleveland before my mother was born. A radical anarchist when it came to political change and a fierce traditionalist when it came to religion and morality, Dorothy frowned on promiscuity. My parents laugh about how one night she accosted my father, coming out of the women's apartment where my mother stayed. Confronting him with a glare as she blocked his path in the hallway, she demanded, "Young man, are your intentions honorable?"

Decades before my parents had met at the soup kitchen on the Bowery, in the earliest years of the movement, a Catholic Worker farm was started — in Newburgh! The first farm, opened in rural Pennsylvania, had failed, and when looking for a new piece of land on which to make another try, Dorothy thought Newburgh would be the perfect location. Not as far from New York City as the farm in Pennsylvania had been, she thought its proximity would encourage more contact between the city houses and farm. Peter Maurin, the other co-founder of the Catholic Worker, spent his last days at Maryfarm in the town of Newburgh, just west of Newburgh the city.

Peter was a French peasant from a farming background whose vision of the Catholic Worker pictured a return to the land. His dream was to relocate homeless or displaced workers onto farming communes, since, as he was fond of repeating, "There is no unemployment on the land." A bioregionalist before the term was invented, Peter eschewed bananas and coffee (among Dorothy's staples) in favor of locally grown foods. He advocated diversified organic agriculture at a time when chemicals and monocrops were taking over as the "modern" way to farm.

When the farm in Newburgh became no longer viable (there weren't enough responsible people to run it), Maryfarm folded. The Second World War had started, and because of the Catholic Worker's staunch pacifist stand, the movement lost many followers. Dorothy would later open yet another farm, but at the time, the closing of Maryfarm represented something of a defeat. Some years later, an overgrown community would amass at the next Catholic Worker farm, in Tivoli, across the river from Newburgh to the north. Close to the train line, on the side of the river that allows passenger cars, Tivoli proved an (almost too) accessible getaway for guests from New York City. My mother and brother and I lived there briefly while my father served jail time for burning his draft card.

After we had moved to Newburgh, we visited the abandoned site of Maryfarm. My parents had pieced together the clues to its location from accounts given by the old-timers who had lived there. As they walked its land, my parents mused about what the property must have looked like when it was inhabited. We came across the caved-in in-ground swimming pool; the goat pen had been nearby. The buildings no longer stood, but my parents guessed where they must have been. After we moved away, that whole area of the town was developed into housing, shopping areas, and a highway. By the time we returned, the area had been so changed that they could not recognize the property again.

Growing up, my parents' belonging in the Catholic Worker movement provided a backdrop as constant as the mountains and river beyond the limits of the Bluff. In the same way my brother and I took in the panorama that gave place to our days, our parents' commitment formed the context of our lives. Too young to fully understand, we took it for granted as much as the landscape around us. My parents lived in a world in which Mahatmas Gandhi seemed more real than our next-door neighbors. The opinions of peace movement members were more important to them than the perceptions of our neighbors.

The proximity of the Grail at Cornwall, a retreat center located on some fifty acres of woods and meadows, made for another influence. It was staffed by an intentional community belonging to a global women's movement, and the Grail women often invited us to the stone cottage and elegant summer mansion which had been donated along with the property by two spinster sisters.

My father's gregarious personality and my mother's gourmet cooking attracted visitors to our house overlooking the Bluff. On the weekends my father was home, he often brought guests from his international peace organization with him. People from various parts of the country, or from different countries, found respite at this corner of the Hudson. Sometimes Catholic Workers exchanged a few days of their hectic work at soup kitchens or shelters for my parents' genteel hospitality. Housed in the extra attic bedroom, they would spend a day or two enjoying the panorama, eating homemade bread and *salad nicoise* prepared by my mother, and talking endlessly about matters related to the peace movement. To this day I run across people who remember meals and conversations on our front porch.

Yet another type of gathering took place at our house. Encouraged by my father, who saw himself in these working-class white teenagers (most from ethnic backgrounds such as Italian, Irish, or Portuguese), neighborhood kids of high school age found my parents' home a place of hospitality. On warm days they hung around on the porch and in winter formed a circle around the dining room table where they gambled as they played cards. On her visits, my poor grandmother guessed rightly that, although they tried to hide it in her presence, they drank beer, smoked cigarettes, and used foul language.

The presence of so many kinds of people made for an unusual sight in our neighborhood. An unlikely assortment of characters lined up on successive front porches: African-Americans from the South, genteel elderly white Northern ladies, scrappy kids of all colors, street-wise teenagers, and hippie types just passing through. I cringed as our guests tried to be friendly with the neighborhood kids, using their best approximation of street language, even as our neighbors cringed at the revolutionary talk they couldn't help overhearing from the radicals assembled around our picnic table on the front porch.

Some of our neighbors had spent their lives trying to climb *out* of poverty, and now that they had almost escaped, nobody was going to preach to them about its merits. Solidarity meant loyalty to one's family and, by extension, one's people — but stopped there. Although excelling at neighborliness, they had no use for commiserating about the problems of unknown lands. As for non-violence, in this city the strong preyed on the weak. Perhaps because of the valley's history in the Revolutionary War and its proximity to West Point, antiwar talk was taken as unpatriotic. Catholic activist Phil Berrigan (who baptized me) was stationed as a priest in Newburgh during the tumultuous time of the race riots and the Vietnam War. When he gave a talk linking racism and militarism at the local college, he was practically run out of town.

My mother had told me and my brother that we were not to recite the Pledge of Allegiance at school, and if a teacher reprimanded us, he or she could deal with *her*. (Our gentle mother positively bristled as she said this.) My brother and I faced a dilemma. We would not defy our teachers or scandalize our classmates, but at the same time we could not disobey our parents. We found a solution that satisfied these two contradictory sets of authority: holding our hands over our hearts, we simply mouthed the words!

In some ways, I lived a local parallel to my father's activism. Before I was born, he had marched with Martin Luther King Jr.; as an adolescent, I sat on our front porch having my hair cornbraided. While he met with torture victims from Chile or Argentina in the mid-1970s (one of whom he brought that night to our house), muddling through a mixture of Italian and Spanish, I was teaching English to my Peruvian grammar school friend, Sandy. While he traveled to the Middle East, where in his hotel lobby in Beirut a bomb exploded, I was beaten up in the Heights for being caught on the wrong street. My father's prized possessions included a letter from El Salvador's Archbishop Oscar

Romero, written shortly before he was shot to death; in Newburgh, I would view a friend's brother writhing from a bullet wound.

MY LAST RECOLLECTION of Dorothy comes from her funeral. Not so many years after those walks along the Bowery sidewalks or the strolls on the beach, my brother and I had both become teenagers. When Dorothy died, her wake was held at the hospitality house for women where she had lived. As we approached the familiar front door flanked by the iron fence, which in warmer weather would have morning glories growing up its slender bars, a host of people crowded the building's entrance. Once we finally made our way into the throng pressing into the house, I saw that the passages were lined with candles. The din of people conversing (the mood felt more like a family reunion than a wake) abated as we turned into the hallway on the right side of the building to the rooms where Dorothy had lived and where her body was now laid out.

My parents took their turn at the kneeler and then melted into the crowd to visit with old friends, as my brother stood silently against the wall, taking everything in. I took a turn at the kneeler in the candlelit room, where a simple wooden box held the tall, stiffened body. My shadow elongating as I dropped to my knees, I closed my eyes and pressed my forehead into my folded hands, taking in the sweet-smelling pine of the coffin. Pleasantly lulled by the droning of voices outside in the hall, I dropped my head to savor a moment of otherworldliness. The hush held out a strangely appropriate peace at which I grasped eagerly.

After a brief rustling and the sudden rise of excited voices outside the door, a figure reverently entered the room. His countenance imperceptible in the darkened room, he gently approached the coffin. Since I was a skinny teenager, there was plenty of room left on the kneeler, and he knelt at my side. It took me some moments to place the familiar, kindly face now shadowed by sadness; as he made the sign of the cross, finishing by kissing his thumb and index finger, I recognized him suddenly as Cesar Chavez, the founder of the United Farm Workers.

Schooling

> *Pray for the peace of Jerusalem:*
> *"May they prosper who love you.*
> *Peace be within your walls,*
>   *and security within your towers."*
> *For the sake of my relatives and friends*
>   *I will say, "Peace be within you."*
> *For the sake of the house of the Lord our God,*
>   *I will seek your good.*
>
> — *Psalm 122*

Our neighborhood, though more diverse than most of the country, was inclined toward racial divisions, like most of the United States. In typical working-class fashion, its response was to expose prejudices rather than to hide them. It would have been impossible to live a segregated existence on the Bluff; dealing with diversity could not be avoided. This multicultural environment was not a comfortable one. A volatile mix of differences, which even then as kids we knew were related to real issues of power and history, had to be at the same time acknowledged and diffused.

Stereotypes were brought out into the open, usually through ethnic jibes that served as a catharsis. For example, an African-American might mimic Spanish by jabbering nonsensical words, or tease a white kid for being "too stiff" to dance. The kid being teased was expected to defend his or her dignity. Others would witness the verbal sparring (such exchanges never took place apart from a group situation) and let the speaker know if he or she had gone too far. If so, the offender would be branded "prejudiced" and chastised ("that ain't right") by the whole group, ostracized until he or she made an overture of reconciliation.

Basic categories of status ranked "knowing" (being acquainted with) people very high. Having many relatives was even better. The more people one "knew" or was related to, the more prestige one would receive from peers. My brother and I found ourselves at a disadvantage. Since we went to Catholic school, we did not know other kids outside of the neighborhood; worse, we had no other family in the city. As pacifists' kids, we fared poorly in another category of supreme importance: in this rough and tumble environment, the ability to defend one's self physically or verbally took on a paramount importance. One could disarm an opponent through humor (though it must not be done in too self-effacing a manner, since this would invite more harassment), but there was no way to completely avoid the pecking order.

In school, a different sort of prejudice dictated social relationships among students. Probably because the school was not integrated enough to have to take race seriously, all students were treated according to the same rules of social class. Only a handful of us from the neighborhood attended private schools, and because this one was run by the parish to which we belonged and was the least expensive of all the private schools in the area, it was our parents' choice. The other students, whose parents had grown up in Newburgh but who had since moved away, came in from the town of Newburgh or its outlying suburbs.

A strict code of etiquette (made more compelling by the fact that it was unwritten, unspoken, and, thus, unquestioned) placed "bus riders" — meaning the suburban kids — above "walkers," who lived in the inner city. As the grades went higher, this stratification became more pronounced. Interestingly, it took hold more strongly among the girls than the boys; the boys even seemed to idealize the more street-smart among themselves. Boys from the city were supposed to be wilder, tougher, and more athletic than their suburban counterparts. In reality, this stereotype did not prove itself to be true, but at least it served to ease the stigma attached to boys from the city neighborhoods. At lunch, the boys ate together as one group, while for all the years I attended, the more social-minded girls ate in two groups: walkers and bus riders. The two African-American sisters in our class, who lived in the suburbs and whose father worked for IBM, sat in the large group.

Our smaller group, made up of walkers, sometimes included a chunky girl with long blonde hair and bright blue eyes whose stammer and awkward manners made her unattractive. Her mother, a single parent, was the priests' housekeeper. Since her family was regarded as the school's charity case, for spells at a time teachers would force the bus riders to take her in — and even to invite her to the sleepovers to which the rest of us walkers were never invited. But after a few months the teachers' vigilance waned, and she would end up back at our table, crestfallen, once again.

Our permanent group included my friend Karen, whose mother was also a single mom, and who, although painfully shy, impressed us with the panoply of jobs she performed before and after school. She had a tendency to fall in love with older men she met while on her paper route. Another girl from the neighborhood attended Catholic school until her family switched her to public school. Her rambunctious temperament enlivened our interactions. Finally, the group included my friend Sandy, whose family had just immigrated from Peru, and who, when I met her all those years later in church after her daughter's catechism class, reminded me that I had taught her English.

Once in a while when a bus rider was ostracized by the larger group for some offense, she would join us for a few days until the other girls forgave her (in which case, no apology given, she simply rejoined the large group at lunchtime). Unlike the girls in our neighborhood, these suburban girls did not fight physically but instead engaged in petty, intense rivalries or gossip in a circle that was forever being sliced up by cutting remarks. I did not so much mind being left alone, finding treasured companionship in diaspora, but I took offense when our refuge was turned into a time-out for castigated bus riders. Those of us outside the circle were free to treat each other with group loyalty and with solicitous affection. I could count on Karen and Sandy not to make fun of my mother's brown bread sandwiches, which made more crumbs than anyone else's. They could depend on me not to sneer at Sandy's exotic tropical canned juices, or the lunches Karen made for herself and her siblings since her mother could barely seem to hold daily life together.

Some of the other kids in the outlying neighborhood thought we were stuck-up because we went to Catholic school. One year, a young sister, fresh-faced and just out of the novitiate (whom we enjoyed because she loved singing folk Mass songs), invited four students to take an accelerated science course held after school. I hated that lonely trip home after the other walkers had left, at an hour by which the public school kids had gotten home. The young sister could never understand why I tried to dodge out after dismissal, and I was too embarrassed to explain that walking home alone in my school uniform I felt like a moving target. Neighborhood kids were already turf-conscious; any difference that attracted their attention to an outsider could justify harassment — or worse.

ONE SPRING AFTERNOON, Ruby's sister Nicole, my next-door neighbor Janice, and I looked for something to do. Jealous of the boys' absorption in whatever manly project they had taken up, the three of us tried to convince them to include us. Putting our heads together, we came upon a sure-fire way to capture their attention: a bucket of cold water. Each of us chose a boy to douse with her cup. When our would-be playmates, splashed in this undignified manner, turned more angry than we had anticipated, we girls took off up the block to escape their wrath. Leaving the safety of our street, we turned the corner and found ourselves in foreign territory — foreign because although we knew the street's name and location, we didn't belong there.

We had been engaged in a gender battle with the boys from our block, but another rivalry replaced this one. Soon a triangle of girls had surrounded us. They were going to let us know that we had gone beyond boundaries that should not be crossed. They were going to pick one of us to beat up, as an example to the others. They chose me, "the white girl." Their fists doubled, and I cringed in shock as the girls closed in. If it were not for a vigilant teenage girl, a neighbor on our block, I would have been beaten up much worse — but the betrayal was already bad enough. I remembered this bitter lesson years later after I had returned to Newburgh with my own little family: my *ahijado* (godson), recently arrived from Mexico, was beat up along with his brother on the way to school.

Crossings

> *May our sons in their youth*
> *be like plants full grown,*
> *our daughters like corner pillars,*
> *cut for the building of a palace.*
> *— Psalm 144*

As the kids in our neighborhood grew into adolescence, with smaller subsets still converging on summer nights at the Bluff, hormones and music began to stir a new pulse in our teenage bodies. Blaring tunes from boom boxes provided essential background to nocturnal card-playing sessions. The air thickened with flirtations that settled, sometimes inexplicably, on a choice person and then dissipated just as mysteriously when attraction moved on to another candidate. While in earlier times I had clanked out revised Greek myths on my father's huge, cumbersome Hermes manual typewriter in front of the bay windows, the river and mountains at my shoulders, now I hid in my room with a notebook writing dreadful love poems based on imaginary relationships.

During those long summer days on each other's porches, we girls practiced love songs, crooning harmonies worthy of an audience. Ice melting on our tongues, we greased ashy legs and knees with Vaseline and preened our lengthening bodies. My friends and I memorized lyrics of popular love songs by playing records over and over until my mother raised objections, to their repetition as much as to their racy lyrics. As the cohesion of the web of kids that used to congregate along the Bluff dissipated, the cluster of kids from the opposite side of the block began to gain momentum. Angelique's grandmother worked nights at her factory job, and their house became a hangout for neighborhood teenagers. By this time, the intrigues were frankly sexual. Boys and girls paired off in the upstairs bedrooms while downstairs kids milled about, courting clumsily.

When Ruby began going with a boy in high school, several of us girls from the Heights began going across town. The walk was made dangerous (and therefore, more exciting) by the risk that girls from across town would beat us up for being in the wrong neighborhood. Our trips were made more adventurous by the fact that we didn't have our parents' permission. Crossing the main street, Broadway, which divides this small city, we walked to the projects where Ruby's boyfriend lived. I had my first kiss, a singularly unromantic moment with Luanne's tall cousin, of which I remember his chewing gum at my mouth and his knobby knees at my thighs, in the basement boiler room of the projects.

On other nights, these same boys reciprocated by coming up to the Heights. Although we girls never spent enough time to be integrated into the social fabric that dominated their neighborhood across town, the boys came frequently enough that they were absorbed into the group that gathered along the Bluff. For teenagers, the Heights was by no means a peaceful setting, but at least it was better than housing projects, where gangs, drugs, and weapons kept residents in a constant state of defensiveness and fear. Around the time we were sneaking off to the projects, a rumor was circulated that after a killing, the dead body had lain unreported for a week because people were too afraid to report the crime to the police.

It was during this time that our racial differences came to the fore more than ever before. Declaring a crush on someone of a different ethnic background, in fact, inevitably served to provoke a rehashing of the tireless debates on realities and stereotypes. As time went on, peer pressure separated us into more rigidly defined groups. Each year, when kids from the neighborhood left their elementary schools for the two junior high schools, they found that in order to avoid being beaten up they had to align themselves with a clique determined by racial or ethnic identity. The same kids who hung out together in our neighborhood had to go separate ways at school — as if the bonds of camaraderie and shared adventure, laced with the doubly twined threads of racial tension and resolution, had never been forged.

As an adult now, I can trace the lines of patterns that began before I was born, into which my brother and I entered without knowing their history. While we were in grammar school, our neighborhood — indeed, the entire city — was shaken by incidents that took place when we were still quite young.

From November 6 to 10 in 1974, riots erupted in the high school and spilled out into the city at large. A fight had broken out between white and African-American and Latino students in the high school, and when other students jumped in, a full-fledged riot was sparked, which caused days of looting. It was the fifth time violence had rocked this city, which like other urban centers in the country, experienced its share of racial disturbances in the late 1960s and early 1970s. But this riot — which lasted the longest of the five — warranted the calling of a state of emergency.

In the months following, an integrated team of community leaders (most notably clergy) met several times in a joint reflection process as the Human Rights Commission of the City of Newburgh to offer recommendations to the community at large. The areas the commission highlighted for closer attention focused on the dire situation of housing, in which slum landlords, most of whom lived outside of the city, took advantage of renters; police treatment of African-Americans and Latinos and the wider issue of distrust between minority communities and police; the lack of decent jobs that paid a living wage and the failure to integrate youth more successfully into the job market; and the need for ways to diffuse the racial tensions that arose in the public schools.

In 1976, Newburgh made national news again when, after an investigation into the causes of the high school riot, the state mandated an integration order requiring bussing. The state had judged that sixteen of the nineteen elementary and secondary schools were unbalanced racially, making for a volatile setting when the diverse student body reached the upper grades. Some community leaders opposed the order, arguing that separate does not always mean unequal: predominantly African-American students filled neighborhood schools where their parents were more likely to become involved, since they were located within walking distance in familiar territory. Others supported the court order, claiming that minority children would have more access to resources and pointing to the racially motivated violence that ensued at the junior high schools and the high school when children from racially seg-regated grammar schools came together for the first time. Six years of lawsuits and hundreds of thousands of dollars later, the city school district complied. The little girls next door were among the first students to be bussed to magnet schools, where Janice learned such astonishing subjects as Japanese and Letisha took up the flute.

ONCE MY BROTHER had graduated from eighth grade, leaving me with still two more years of grammar school to go, I spent more time on the walk to and from school with girl friends. An-gelique, whose grandmother's house had hosted the neighborhood teenagers' trysts, was a grade above me; Marisol, my best friend, was a grade below me.

Marisol lived with her mother, stepfather, two sisters, and half-sister in a narrow three-story apartment, the basement of which held the kitchen, where we spent most of our time. Marisol's step-father did not work, due to a back injury for which he was forever going to doctor's appointments — with Marisol as a translator (meaning she had to miss school). Her mother and half-sister worked with scores of other women in a clothing factory on a side street at the foot of the Heights. A huge room lit by glar-ing fluorescent bulbs and made deafening by humming machines, the shop was stiflingly hot in summer. Like Marisol's mother and half-sister, most of the women who worked the machines were immigrant women and women of color.

Being recently arrived from Puerto Rico, Marisol's family did not have difficulty with legal status, but struggled with culture shock. Suspicious of her friends, Marisol's parents severely re-stricted her social life. They were terrified of African-Americans (of whom they knew only stereotypes) and reluctant to mix with whites (whom they had to deal with out of necessity but who shouldn't be trusted). By sending their daughters to Catholic school, Marisol's parents hoped to mitigate the negative influ-ence of the new society in which they found themselves. They found the United States morally lax, its children disrespectful and its teenagers promiscuous. Television confirmed their worst fears about this country while language differences impeded them from forming friendships with people living here who might have dispelled their worries. Marisol was rarely allowed to come to my house. If she were, she had to be accompanied by her two younger sisters and, worse, chaperoned by her resentful half-sister.

Of a generous nature, boisterous and athletic, Marisol was blessed with a cheerful, outgoing personality. She chafed under her stepfather's overprotectiveness. Permission even to go to the corner store had to be fought for. When they used to argue she would shout, "You're not my real father!" and though he understood enough English to be infuriated by this, he could make no response.

Marisol's mother was appealed to, but she refused to openly take sides in the tug-of-war between her husband and Marisol. She made her quiet distrust of their new surroundings known more passively, keeping a "Miraculous Hand" candle lit — especially when her girls went out — as a protection against the evil that lurked at random in this new land to which they had moved. On the morning after I had slept over, when Marisol's stepfather followed me into the bathroom and ran his palm over the fabric of my nightgown, I realized that danger lurked inside and not just outside the house.

Exodus

Marisol and her sisters went to Catholic school, but their family's religiosity combined practices from eclectic sources. At that time, Catholic pastoral ministry to Latinos in the area was still in its early stages. Although in 1975, an article in the *New York Times* speculated that Newburgh held a large population of New York's Latinos, second in percentage only to New York City, and already by 1977, a bilingual education conference was held by the public school system, their presence went virtually unnoticed. It took a dynamic priest from the other side of Broadway — stationed at the parish to which my husband and I now belong — to awaken the church to the city's Latino presence.

In the meantime, people like Marisol's parents sought to live out their faith life using various sources. At home, they continued to practice *Santería*-based customs, in which Catholic and African beliefs converged. For example, specific offerings (particular foods, colored candles or objects) were placed before statues or other holy images to protect the family's well-being or to petition for favors. Outside of the home, they found the parish where we attended school cold and unwelcoming. More definitively, it offered no Spanish Mass. Marisol's family began to attend, instead, the Primera Asamblea de Dios, a Pentecostal Protestant church with a small, vivacious congregation. The numbers of adherents seemed tiny in that huge building built for white Protestants whose fellowship had, by now, withered, but they managed to fill the building with enthusiasm. Attracted by its expressive worship style, lively music (with electric instruments, no less), and the availability of services and activities during the week, they enjoyed its close feeling of community. Devotionalism and music predominated over ritual or written prayers — even though its members claimed to be more biblically based than Catholics. Many members of Marisol's parents' generation were illiterate, while many of Marisol's own generation had been brought up more literate in English than in their maternal tongue. At one small midweek service for girls and women I found myself, a fourteen-year-old with three months' high school Spanish, sounding out the scriptural passage — not understanding what I was reading — because no one else present could read Spanish.

Tagging along with the families of my friends, I could slip into a crowd more easily than an adult could have. In addition to accompanying Marisol's family to the Primera Asamblea de Dios, sometimes I went with Angelique, her younger brother and sisters, and their grandmother to the House of Refuge on Broadway. The vibrancy of this Pentecostal storefront church, with its rocking music, interactive sermons, and intensely social atmosphere offset its negatives: girls were not supposed to wear pants or makeup (inside *or* outside of the church — Angelique hid from "church ladies" in public if she had trespassed these rules). Visiting preachers were sometimes women, something foreign to my church experience. And while women did as much of the work as in our Catholic parish — directing the choir, organizing the many social events, and ushering the services — in this storefront church male preachers seemed to take them more seriously.

As the only white person in the assembly, I felt shy, especially during the potlucks that took place after worship. But more than that, I was fascinated and a little frightened by spirit possession. Sometimes during the services, the drumming and clapping would reach an ecstatic pitch — and then keep on going. Sweat dripped on faces and stained underarms as the room steamed with heat and bodies moved to the music. Just when one would think that the intensity couldn't go on climbing, the music intertwined with preaching would hit another height and at least one worshiper would be "filled with the Holy Spirit." Angelique's grandmother seemed to hope my friend would be among those who swooned and spoke in tongues, but to my relief, she stayed at my side, clapping along with the rest of the congregation.

At the House of Refuge the exodus story came alive. In class, of course, we learned Bible stories from the Polish order of Sisters who ran our school with their descriptive retellings of Old Testament myths and sagas. Taken from the Hebrew Bible, these passages, presented to us in harmonized versions as literal happenings, were made understandable to us children at a fundamental moral level. However, I must admit that the stories captured our attention mostly because they were shrouded in the allure of mystery. Drawn by the young's natural affinity with the miraculous, our imaginations were awakened — as indeed they must have been awakened around campfires thousands of years ago. (Studying Scripture in graduate school, I am constantly surprised at how much the symbolic worldview the Sisters imparted to us helps me enter the mentality of the biblical writers.)

But at the House of Refuge, biblical symbolism was not only taken for granted as truth belonging to the past; it was *worked with in the present* to interpret God's saving actions in our contemporary setting. Only as an adult witnessing base ecclesial communities in Latin America did I come to understand what I had intuitively grasped years earlier in this storefront church on Broadway in Newburgh.

The preacher's sonorous voice thumped as he laid out a modern scene of how the Exodus would take place. Punctuated by sighs, shouts, or refrains from the congregation — who responded in one voice — the preacher enumerated: "Someone has a phone bill, Lord, it needs to be paid. Someone's in the hospital, Lord, who needs to be healed. Someone's on drugs, Lord, and can't find their way out of slavery. Someone lost their job, Lord, they need your mercy. Someone's getting evicted, Lord, find them a new home." With music providing a background for his voice, the preacher implored, demanded, and expressed gratitude in turns. The assembly would be on its feet, echoing his petitions. This went on for quite some time, but the most amazing thing about it was not the persistence with which the petitions were made but rather the assurance with which they were closed. God had done wonders before. God would do so now.

Looking back with the eyes of an adult, only now do I realize that the subtext of racial discrimination provided the framework for this congregation's experiencing itself as a people in exodus. Many members of the older generations, among them Angelique's grandmother and our neighbors at Dolly's house, had migrated from the Carolinas or Virginia. For them, sharecropper families, slavery was a living memory. In my research into the city's past, I learned that slavery had existed in Newburgh, too (the famous abolitionist Sojourner Truth was born in Ulster County, just north), and in the local public library's archives one can find — along with records of livestock registered by settler families — the annals of slaves owned in the area. The racism my friends' families experienced in Northern cities was just a different version of what they had come from. They were fond of saying, "In the South, white people don't care how close you get, as long as you don't get too high. In the North, they don't care how high you get, as long as you don't get too close."

As a foundational text for Jews and Christians, the exodus story provides us with a starting point for reflection on who we are as peoples as well as a mythologized account of our past. As New Testament scholars point out, Jesus' life and ministry cannot be understood without reference to the great exodus event. The Passover supper Jesus celebrated with his followers, a Seder meal, elucidates the entire content of Christ's identity and ministry, made ongoing through time by our participation in eucharistic community.

As biblical scholars began to apply modern methods of inquiry to the exodus narratives and as archeological discoveries added excitement to the search for biblical contexts, theories about "the world behind the texts" began to take shape. (Our own grammar school teachers, swept up in the euphoria but lacking the scholarly background to judge its wilder claims, ignited our young minds with archeological certainties such as the discovery of Noah's Ark.) Recognizing that biblical accounts were often written centuries after the events described were supposed to have taken place, and understanding more critically the role that such foundational texts would have played in Hebrew society, scholars began to offer more intellectually challenging and historically nuanced interpretations.

While biblical scholars have come to an impasse in trying to flesh out a historical-critical context for the exodus narratives, it is generally agreed that the texts offer theologically mature reflections concerned not with the historicity of actual events but rather their religious meaning for Israel. Three strands of hypotheses have been proposed regarding the historical origin of the Exodus.

The first, the Conquest model, coincides with the version told in Joshua 1–12. It suggests that Israel's occupation of Canaan took place as a military conquest under the unified leadership of the twelve tribes descended from Jacob's sons, accomplished in one military campaign that destroyed cities and expelled Canaanite tribes. This model has come under scrutiny with archeological discoveries that challenge the straightforward character of its assertions. For example, Jericho, a small fort rather than a large city at the time of its conquest, was not actually destroyed, just taken over. And scholars generally agree that the number of Israelites who fled Egypt was probably much smaller than we had previously envisioned. The existence of the twelve tribes as based on a kinship relation of twelve brothers is now widely taken to be a symbolic representation of disparate ethnic groups being brought into a new self-understanding as a single people.

The second, the Infiltration model, proposes that the occupation of the land took place not primarily through military means, but rather through a long process that culminated in the armed triumph of King David. As nomads who migrated into Palestine, this theory proposes, Israelites coexisted alongside their Canaanite neighbors, gradually mingling through intermarriages and taking over "turf" through more peaceful means. In this model, military confrontation took place when Israelite agriculturalists and pastoralists (along with their Canaanite neighbors and allies) confronted the urban city-states that dominated the rural areas. This theory may be partially true, as biblical texts do support some of its assertions, such as intermarriage, alliances, or conversion (e.g., Rahab at the fall of Jericho). It emphasizes that Canaanites were allowed to join the sociopolitical religion of Israel or to become allies in small-scale military operations undertaken by individual tribes.

The third hypothesis, called the Revolt model, suggests that the destruction of Canaanite cities took place from within. Casting rural Canaanites as full-fledged protagonists alongside the Israelites, the Revolt model proposes that a small band of Yahwists recently escaped from Egypt sparked a rebellion against urban oppressors. Noting that the tributary system had made the city-states rich at the expense of impoverished and subjugated peasants, this hypothesis speculates that the true identity of Israel emerged as a mingling of Canaanite and Israelite peoples, united under their monotheistic belief in Yahweh and brought together by their shared experience of rural oppression.

However the Exodus actually took place, its narratives tell an astounding truth. An enslaved people empowered by the one, true God left their oppression behind. Led by a bicultural prophet (Moses, after all, was raised as a prince in Pharaoh's court), they stepped forward on a journey into the unknown to forge a new identity. In this covenant, social barriers were broken as men, women, and children — an entire people — stood at Sinai. While racially speaking the Israelites were not a distinct ethnic group, in the exodus tradition they became a single family.

Suddenly free of oppressors, the people had to develop their own leadership. Whereas before they had suffered under others, now they had to endure the consequences of their quest for free-dom, like thirst in the desert or the uncertainty of the journey. In accepting these consequences, they would learn to depend on God alone. A chosen people, they had to learn to choose their own destiny. Only in doing so with faithfulness would they be an inspiration to others who suffered oppression, a blessing to all peoples and a light to the nations. Before entering the Promised Land, the people had to undergo a desert sojourn and a series of testing. They were being tried by fire.

"Migrants"

> The Lord is the strength of the people;
>   God is the saving refuge of the anointed.
> O save your people, and bless your heritage;
>   be their shepherd, and carry them forever.
>   — Psalm 28

Neither my brother nor I had been born yet when it happened, but we were affected while growing up in Newburgh by the con-sequences of a scandal that had long-lasting implications for the city's race relations. In the years 1960 to 1962, the city manager, Joseph Mitchell, launched an aggressive campaign. Claiming that

5 percent of the city's population was dependent on welfare and that 20 to 30 percent of all births at Newburgh's hospital were illegitimate, Mitchell unloosed a public torrent of fears. He convinced alarmed citizens that Newburgh was being overrun by delinquents, that its fiscal budget was being eaten up by social services, and that the lazy, undeserving poor were flooding in from all over the country to collect welfare payments. Newburgh's prosperity was being preyed upon by outsiders who did not belong. In a word, those to blame were "migrants."

Confusion reigned while Newburgh citizens debated the substance of the pillars of Mitchell's platform. In actuality, less than 3 percent of the population received any form of governmental assistance. An amazed spokesperson from St. Luke's Hospital wondered out loud how Mitchell had arrived at the percentage of illegitimate births since the hospital kept no record of the marital status of newborns' parents. Religious leaders — quick to recognize the racial bias in Mitchell's claims — defended the city's newcomers and sought to clarify the points by which he had aroused the public.

Playing on Newburgh's self-perception as an "all-American city" (during the 1950s, as Newburgh rode the crest of post–World War II manufacturing, it was awarded this title by a popular magazine), Mitchell had awakened residents' very real fears that the city was going downhill, fast. By 1961, the nonwhite population had reached 16 percent — an unthinkably high proportion for whites who had never had to come "too close" to people of other backgrounds. Lured by the promise of factory jobs, African-American families from the South and a handful of families from Puerto Rico settled in Newburgh. In many cases, family members or friends from their home community had found their way to Newburgh as seasonal fruit pickers and returned with stories about this small city with plentiful employment opportunities in the scenic Hudson Valley.

But workers were coming in just as industry was beginning to move out. The slow drain on the local economy had begun. From an all-time high of thirty-five thousand inhabitants in the

1950s, the city's population in 1960 had already begun to dip, to thirty-one thousand during Mitchell's term. Residents were already beginning to feel anxious about their city's future. In 1962, the documentary movie *The Battle of Newburgh*, filmed at the height of the controversy, exposed a city fraught with racial tensions, an already faltering economy, and a crisis in self-identity.

Capitalizing on the underlying fears that lay below the surface of Newburgh's changing reality, Mitchell proposed his own solution to the "welfare problem." Snubbing the federal government, he introduced his own thirteen-point proposal, which, he claimed, would weed out the undeserving from the deserving poor. Those who were entitled to assistance would have to pick up their payments at the police station. On the first payment distribution day of the new system, reporters noted with disgust the trickle of war veterans, widows with small children, and disabled factory workers in an overwhelmingly white line of recipients — hardly the droves of "migrants" Mitchell had forecast. The federal government stepped back in charge of the welfare system, the controversy faded, and soon afterward Mitchell retired to Florida after being accused of accepting bribes for the building of the Chadwick apartment complex.

Newburgh's story had drawn national attention because it epitomized in vivid, encapsulated form a struggle being played out in various settings all over the country. Its small size and scenic backdrop made an ideal stage for portraying issues of urban crisis, while the exaggerated claims and vociferous personality of the city manager made him a theatrical character. The African-American leadership (notably, its clergy) cut its teeth in forging alliances with local supporters and defending its constituency, an experience that would serve them well in later civil rights struggles. For Newburgh as a whole, however, the episode had sown seeds of racial distrust and suspicion that would bear lasting, bitter fruit. As recently as 1990, the Ku Klux Klan burned a cross on a lawn in Newburgh.

The deepest irony of the Battle of Newburgh fiasco is that the gruesome picture Mitchell painted, of a ruined city overrun by delinquency, has come true. Over 40 percent of the county's total welfare budget is spent here. The annual per capita of Newburgh residents comes to about $8,000 a year, as compared to the county's average figure of almost double that amount, $15,000. Two exodus crossings have taken place: In the first, migrants fled the poverty and desperation of the rural South to make Newburgh their home. In the second, those who had lived here long enough to enter the middle class moved away, leaving the city forsaken. In the Hudson Valley, our city has the reputation of a violent, drug-ridden, dangerous place to live.

While Mitchell laid his finger on the pulse of the changing demographic patterns (Newburgh's white population is now the "minority"), he was dead wrong about where to lay the blame for Newburgh's economic and social woes. Mitchell's "migrants," who came from the Carolinas and Virginia, like Dolly and Garrett, were hard-working low-paid laborers who filled factory jobs, packed church pews, and began converting their hard-earned dollars into owner-occupied houses (paying taxes all along). It was their children's generation who either "made it" in to the eyes of society through education and hard work — and then, like their white counterparts, moved out — or stayed behind (like the kids who gathered around my family's table playing cards), prone to a spectrum of despair. However, unlike their white counterparts, boosted along their upwardly mobile trajectory by privileges due to their skin color, African-Americans had to counter racial discrimination, both overt and subtle, the whole way.

Coming to Newburgh at the particular elbow of time at which we did, my family was privileged to meet members of that noble generation, the founding men and women who had braved the unknown exodus journey to establish their families in Newburgh. They may have come from far away, but they belonged now to the city on the banks of a river that flows both ways.

Angelique's grandmother, along with others of her generation, had traversed a different type of desert in search of a better life for her children. Coming up from the rural South in search of a new homeland, she thought she had found it in New York City.

Instead she lost her daughter to drug addiction. Moving again, to this small city on the banks of the Hudson, across the river from a scenic mountain range, she hoped Newburgh would make a more promising home for her grandchildren. While our Catholic school teachers had convincingly shown us a map of the forty-year trek in the desert, pointing out where the sea had parted and where Moses received the Ten Commandments, most biblical scholars maintain that the river and the mountain that figure so prominently in the exodus story cannot be identified with certainty. In at least one living enactment of the exodus narratives in contemporary setting, I have no doubt.

Interpreting their own history through the lens of biblical salvation history, the congregation of Angelique's church, the House of Refuge, actually relived the Exodus. Not *in spite of* but precisely *because of* their communal history of oppression, they were God's Chosen People. Mainstream society might lambast them from all sides as inferior, and well-intentioned liberal whites might portray them as victims, but inside those walls they were the anointed ones who could accept God's saving power and also bear God's message to others. Each family there knew too well the costs of turning away from this promise of liberation. To "lose the faith" was to abandon all hope. Angelique's mother was conspicuously absent, as were the fathers of her four children. But if the families came together to remember their history of oppression, to name the causes of their suffering, and to cross through it, as their fore-bears in faith had walked through the Red Sea and wandered through the desert, they could rekindle the promise that might yet save a whole people.

Three

Witness

Luanne's mother lived a block or two beyond the House of Refuge, just shy of Broadway, on a side street cluttered with trash. Periodically Luanne went to visit, and so I thought nothing of it when one morning she announced that she had to go home and check in on her family (I must have been about twelve years old at the time.) When she invited me to go along, an invitation that I accepted, Luanne warned me, "My mother's house ain't like your house. Don't you dare make fun of it or I'll pound you. That's my mom's." After her chores at Dolly's house were done, we set off.

Arriving at the house, we seated ourselves on the couch in the living room while Luanne's mother asked about the health of each of the relatives at Dolly's. Other family members or friends came in and out casually while they were talking; Luanne's mother kept a busy house. The oldest brother of the family came in from fishing at the river with a bucket of catfish he had caught. As he cleaned the fish in the kitchen, some of which still squirmed under his knife, and as the room cleared of other visitors, Luanne got to the point: How was her brother? She had heard he had been shot. I sat riveted, as surprised by the news as by their mother's response. After briefly lamenting her son's poor judgment in choosing company, Luanne's mother said, "Go upstairs and see for yourself."

I followed cautiously up to the mysterious second story. The landlord charged her mother rent for the first floor and then pretended not to know that they inhabited the abandoned one above, as well. Several steps were missing, and a beam came down from somewhere in the ceiling across the top of the stairwell. Chunks of floor and wall gaped open. The bathroom fixtures stood in obvious disrepair, though from its dripping faucet, the shower appeared to be in use. Windows covered over, the upper story of the house filled our eyes with darkness. Making our way to the bedroom with its half-open door, we heard a low groan.

Terrified, I could only peek in at the bed, a platform with a mattress. In his late teens or at most early twenties, Luanne's brother lay with his upper body exposed and a bloodstained sheet covering his lower body. As if delirious, he responded summarily to Luanne's questions, his voice sounding as if it came from far-away. No, it didn't hurt much. He would not go to the hospital since a gunshot wound would have to be reported to police. No, there was nothing she could do for him. Finally we went back downstairs to where the house had once again filled with guests and the catfish were being prepared for dinner.

Over the next weeks I heard that Luanne's brother had gotten better. The bullet had been taken out, though I never learned who had done it or where. Like her warning issued before the visit, Luanne had handed me a stern word of advice on the walk home: better not say anything about what I had seen and heard.

NEWBURGH, THEN, holds the origin of memory. Here I tasted chitterlings and iced tea sweetened beyond recognition of any beverage my mother would have served. Here my ear became attuned to the words for vegetables I could not yet name, foods whose names I could hardly pronounce. Here I learned the solidarity of neighborliness even as we grew into the knowledge of race and class distinctions that undercut it. Here we had shared the bread of poverty without fully realizing we were poor, so sweet and fulfilling had been its companionship. Here we witnessed, conversely, its power to break young bodies, to tear into a skin's flesh like a bullet into silk. Here we had stood, a line of raggedy kids with ashy knees, along the grassy precipice of the Bluff, waving to the solid metal body of a train thundering into the dark tunnel, or to the full white sails of the *Clearwater* passing by on tranquil waters.

Estuary

As I studied the city's history, clues to the past kept surprising me. Perhaps the greatest surprises, however, came not from the recorded history of the its people's failures and achievements, but from the natural evolution of the land and river. The Hudson River flows into the wide mouth of an estuary that covers an area from just above Newburgh to New York City. A semi-enclosed body of water with free connection to the ocean, an estuary makes an ideal habitat for the sea's young. In scientific terms, the estuary creates a nutrient trap that impedes the flushing of planktonic organisms out of the lower estuary. In more understandable terms, the estuary acts as a gigantic nursery: it allows newly hatched fish to develop, fed on plentiful nutrients, until they grow large enough to fend for themselves.

Blue crab, carp, killifish, anchovy, herring, white perch, tom-cod, striped bass, sturgeon, oysters, clams, and a host of others depend on the estuary for survival. Safe from falling prey to the larger fish of the open sea, the young feed on the rich micro-scopic organisms of the river bottom. Since the river water flows both ways, it holds decomposing leaves and vegetation more than would water flowing in just one direction. The young find plenty on which to feed.

Unlike the ocean's harsher salt water, the river's low salinity rate around Newburgh allows vulnerable young fish to become accustomed to salt water that will become their home. Even apart from lunar tidal cycles, an estuary's waters are in perpetual motion. Friction between salt and fresh water produces movement. Surface waters flow south while salt water flows inland from the ocean, causing dual tide direction. Contrary tides tug the many species of the river's young back and forth, north and south, and then back again in a rocking motion, as if the riverbed were a giant aquatic cradle. This lulling motion fulfills another purpose: it introduces the young fish gradually to the direction they will travel. Making their way south, most will eventually leave the relative safety of the estuary to enter the open sea.

ON OUR FIRST VISIT back as a family, on the occasion of the ordination anniversary of the priest who began pastoral ministry
to Latinos in this city, my parents, brother, and I drove into
Newburgh from Connecticut. It was a few years since we had
moved away. I was soon to graduate from high school, and my
brother had already done so. My father's job with a local coun-
cil of churches and my parents' work running a Catholic Worker
House of Hospitality kept them absorbed in our new setting, but
we had all wished to satisfy the nostalgia awakened by the priest's
invitation. As we approached the city on the busy thoroughfare
that runs along the river banks, soon Storm King rose majestically before us; Bannerman's Island came into view. We opened
car windows to the river's familiar, salty smell and to the high-
pitched cries of seagulls. Mt. Beacon stood implacable as always
across the water, which that day crashed energetically, topped
by frothing white breakers. But the huge, haunting train tunnel,
which enticed us with its cool, dank interior on sweltering summer afternoons, against whose sooty walls we had flattened our
backs and palms, was gone. It had been razed as a danger spot.

What first surprised me and my brother was how small it
looked — what used to be our whole world. In the blink of an eye
we crossed the creek where so often my brother and his friends had
gone fishing (and where he had yanked my head above the rank
waters), on whose banks they had scavenged leftovers dumped by
factories. The chain of houses on our block, already visible above
the road, looked like a short row of ordinary, dilapidated buildings that could be taken in by one sole glance. We found the ride
between our house and the old school unrecognizably short, in
comparison with the long, dreaded walk of childhood. The grammar school was about to be closed, like so many other inner-city
Catholic parish schools.

Though we could not go into our old house since it was rented
to tenants, we noted its deteriorated condition (little did we guess
how much worse it would be in later years). At that time, our
elderly neighbors were still alive, and we visited each of them.
Mayor Mickey still kept watch in the neighborhood. Dolly's roses,

tended by Garrett's faithful hand, bloomed fragrant as ever. The most notable changes had taken place in the young.

The mother of the two once-little girls next door had had another baby, this one (finally) a boy. She had given up her own place across town and now lived in the attic apartment. Ruby and Nicole's family had already moved from their house around the corner to a home in the suburbs. In a reversal of "settling out," Luanne had gone to live at the farm where she worked packing apples and married a migrant farmworker from Florida. The boy on whom my affections had most consistently rested had joined the army along with five others from the group that used to converge on the Bluff. My friend Angelique was pregnant and hadn't finished high school. Her grandmother now kept her sequestered away from her former friends. Like her, Marisol had gotten pregnant. Her family decided they'd had enough and they had left, moving back to Puerto Rico. I never saw either of them again.

The neighborhood seemed strangely empty and unfamiliar, although a gaggle of young children (I didn't know any of them) lined up along the grassy precipice to wave to the trains charging past and the sailboats gliding by, just as we had done.

As changed as the Heights appeared, the commercial areas shocked me the most. A department store, the last of the prominent businesses along lower Broadway, had finally packed it in. The old theater building, used as a movie cinema while we lived here, had been abandoned. The Single Room Occupancy hotel above it appeared as unsavory as ever. Driving down Broadway, I saw with new eyes the boarded up storefronts, battered old buildings, garbage-strewn sidewalks, and pocked side streets.

The ancient Dutch Reformed church, the historical landmark designated for a cultural center through our tenant's community organizing, stood forlorn. Its elegant Romanesque pillars presided over a crumbling structure the same as before. (Just as we were leaving Newburgh, our tenant's dream had come close to being realized. An Opening Night concert had even been held as a fundraiser. But after we moved, we learned, the entire project disintegrated amid accusations over funding — countered by the organizers' charges of racist treatment. The plans unraveled in bitterness.)

Driving past the women's shelter my neighbors had helped to start, I noticed the house looked neglected. Although the building seemed to be in use, it appeared in need of the same tender loving care we had put into it so many years ago. Pallets of bags of white bread had been dumped, literally, on the sidewalk, beside garbage bags of clothes half-spilled out. Aimless passersby browsed the contents and picked through the bread, leaving the mess even more shabby and unkempt.

On the other side of the river stood IBM, the place of work that had employed so many of my classmates' parents and that shone during my childhood like a beacon of the American Dream itself. Since we had moved, the company's local workforce had plummeted. From its height of over 32,200 employees in the 1980s, it had crashed to about 13,100 employees in 1993. By the time of our visit the layoffs had begun.

Though Newburgh had sunk to its lowest population (23,500) while we were living there, its economy stagnating, suburban sprawl continued to mushroom outside its city limits. On this visit, the other reality that surprised us was that — in spite of IBM's layoffs — the areas outside the city seemed more populated and more developed than ever. A pocket of impoverished inner city tucked in a surrounding area of prosperity, Newburgh had been, literally, abandoned. Its infrastructure still relatively intact, it had been forgotten by the upwardly mobile who left. Unrealized at the time, this abdication had created an opening for newcomers to the river's banks.

FOR HIS ORDINATION ANNIVERSARY, the priest rented a cruise ship and threw a party on board. We parked our car with its Connecticut plates at the docks and embarked with the other guests. Riding up and down the river on the *Dayliner*, entertained by a *salsa* band and *mariachis* in turn, we swept our eyes over the familiar, beloved river banks from a new vantage point. The grassy ledge of the Bluff in plain view, we watched for our old street as the boat sailed past. Other faces in the crowd, parishioners from the church where Kenney and I would make a home so many years later, already indicated new life in the city.

Just as my family had writhed during those two years with the stress of my father's not being able to find decent employment, just as we were forced to turn over the mortgage for our home, recent arrivals had come in search of jobs and housing. Already a handful of immigrants had come from Argentina, Cuba, Mexico, Peru, the Dominican Republic, Honduras to join the already numerous Puerto Rican city residents; these pioneers laid the tracks for others who would follow in later years. Members of the Human Rights Commission had already made an observation in the report issued after those last, most destructive riots that undocumented immigrants being taken advantage of by slum landlords were afraid to report housing violations for fear of themselves being reported to the authorities. The report's suggested response? "To diligently seek out and report aliens illegally residing in the city."

True, it was at about that time that Newburgh elected the first African-American woman mayor for a city of its size, a sign of hope; but she governed a city whose population had been shrinking steadily since the Mitchell controversy. Middle-class families had been moving out into the suburbs, leaving gaps in jobs and housing. Hidden among these figures, evident only to people like this forward-thinking priest who started Catholic ministry to Latin American immigrants, was a silent presence that multiplied yet remained invisible to public eyes. Newburgh had once again started to grow.

In the county, the percentage increase in the Latino population seventeen years of age and older since 1990 was calculated in the census as 98 percent. In the non-Latino population, the same age group's increase measured only 8 percent. The handful of pioneers who set anchor here bridged the way for others. For example, the first Argentines arrived in Newburgh a good thirty years ago, but a significant influx did not take place until Argentina's economy crashed last year. Now one comes across Argentines with their elegantly accented Spanish each morning in the Italian bakery on Broadway before they take off for construction or factory jobs.

Newburgh-born young people leave for work, attracted to better jobs in bigger cities, or to settle down, drawn to suburban areas where they prefer to raise their own children. But those who come here as recent arrivals most often come precisely *as the young.* Unlike the non-Latino population, where women outnumber men, there are more men than women; the higher numbers reflect a workforce where young people, disproportionately males, risk immigration in search of work.

Often the most talented and the most enterprising are those who brave a new landscape. Perhaps, like my husband's friend who holds a law degree but works picking apples, they do not have the family connections or wealth to compete in a corrupt sector of their country. Perhaps unskilled laborers realize that in a factory in New York they can earn wages several times what they would earn working the same job in a *maquiladora* (sweatshop) back home. Others of more humble backgrounds exchange one countryside for another, leaving their own crops untended to pick someone else's. The city that cannot hold the children of its own shores has become a Promised Land for the young of others.

It is the young who are nurtured here; it is the young who leave here. On the deck of the *Dayliner,* coasting past the ruins of Bannerman's Island to the music of a *salsa* band and *mariachis,* I glimpsed a flowering of Newburgh just beginning to take place on the shore. As the city receives new waves of immigrants at their prime, the young begin once again to make their way to its banks.

Captivity

On winter evenings, my mother sat at her sewing machine in the dining room in front of the fireplace, making clothes for us or working on the intricate squares of leftover fabric scraps that became multicolored quilts envied by her hippie friends. My memory of her, intent over her sewing at the great round table, turns melancholy at the close of our years in Newburgh.

When my father lost his job with the international peace organization for which he worked, my family entered a downward spiral. The stream of visitors from the peace movement and the Catholic Worker slowed to a trickle. While I was partly relieved at not having to explain to provincially minded friends or neighbors who was at our house *this* time, there were no guests to lift my parents' lugubrious mood. Until now, although my mother always had to scrape together the money to pay bills, we had never had utilities turned off. My brother and I wore hand-me-down school uniforms, but each year, we had to have new shoes; my mother's anxiety when shopping for them now became palpable.

That first September of my family's troubles, I chose a pair of honey-brown lace-up shoes that I loved for their embroidered design across the top. Each day the ribbon of embroidery looked up at me reproachingly, until I no longer felt joy in their beauty but rather guilt at having added to my mother's worries.

I knew what poverty in Newburgh *looked* like. Our neighbors depended on an intricate and precariously held together network of food stamps, welfare benefits, and low-paying, unstable jobs in the service industry or manufacturing. Relatives often swapped goods such as clothes or household items and exchanged services such as childcare or handyman jobs because they couldn't otherwise afford them. Luanne's brother fished not just because it was his hobby, but to put dinner on the table. And once while staying overnight at the little girls' stiflingly hot attic apartment, I remember opening the refrigerator to find nothing in there except a half-dozen eggs and a pitcher of water.

But this was having a taste of what poverty *felt* like. It's like swimming in place with your head just at the surface, watching everything, but not being able to rise out of the water. It's like holding your breath all the time, even when you exhale, as if your lungs have to wait indefinitely to expand again. It's living in the moment, not able to think beyond the present, because tomorrow, anything might happen.

In a periodically repeated ritual, one of the Sisters would pull me out of the classroom to whisper in the hallway, as if it were an illicit subject, "Has your father found a job yet?" When I replied in the negative, she would inevitably sigh, and I could not help but feel that I had let her down. Her words, uttered in a low voice and rote as a formula, "We'll keep praying," served as my dismissal to return to the classroom. After two years during which we had friends' and neighbors' sympathies (some of their families had been through worse bouts of unemployment), we did what we had to do in a reversal of the exodus people arriving to the Promised Land. We left.

> O God, the nations have come into your inheritance;
>> they have defiled your holy temple;
>> they have laid Jerusalem in ruins.
> They have given the bodies of your servants
>> to the birds of the air for food,
>> the flesh of your faithful to the wild animals of the earth.
> They have poured out their blood like water
>> all around Jerusalem,
>> and there was no one to bury them.
> We have become a taunt to our neighbors,
>> mocked and derided by those around us.
>> — Psalm 79

The major portions of the Old and New Testaments (or in more interfaith-appropriate terms, the Hebrew Bible and the Christian Testament) were written in the shadow of the destruction of the First and Second Temples. The city of Jerusalem — named, ironically, a "city of peace" — was razed both times, first by the Babylonians, then by the Romans. At the time of the first destruction, the Northern Kingdom had already fallen to conquerors. Prophets had warned the Southern Kingdom that the same would happen if Yahweh's laws went ignored. But in 587 B.C.E., Jerusalem fell to the Babylonians.

In an equivalent to contemporary Third World "brain drain," the young, the nobles, and the educated were forcibly removed from their homeland and taken in captivity. Having seen their beloved city sacked by invaders and left in ruins, they were led away to administer to the empire that had conquered them. While many served as scribes or in other professional capacities, and thus never suffered slavery in the same way as their ancestors of the Exodus, their dream of return echoed the ancient promise of liberation.

The irony of the Exile is that, without it, the Hebrew Bible as we know it might never have been compiled. During their years as strangers in a foreign land, having the freedom of the Exodus eclipsed by the captivity of Exile, the Jews (their new name derived from "Judah") were forced to reflect upon and codify their communal faith experience. Written texts were reread in light of their current experience; oral narratives not yet written down were set to scrolls. The experience of the Exodus was recalled, taking on even more poignancy for a people again enslaved far from their homeland. Forced to revisit the origins of their identity, the exiles had to record their history and articulate their beliefs if they were to pass on the faith to their children in a hostile gentile environment.

Written during the Exile, Psalm 137 laments,

> *By the rivers of Babylon —*
>> *there we sat down and there we wept*
>> *when we remembered Zion.*
> *On the willows there*
>> *we hung up our harps.*
> *For there our captors*
>> *asked us for songs,*
>> *and our tormentors asked for mirth, saying,*
>> *"Sing us one of the songs of Zion!"*

The song continues by asking, "How could we sing the Lord's song in a foreign land?" This psalm sings of a refusal to sing. Written, it allows the author to make a bold statement: "If I forget you, O Jerusalem, may my right hand wither!" If the scribe who wrote down this psalm forgets the people's suffering, not only will his writing hand have not served its purpose; it will have betrayed its purpose. Remembering is, in itself, an act of defiance.

THE CHILLING TEMPERATURES of New Hampshire, for that was where we moved, accentuated the cold grip on my heart. I was fourteen years old; my brother, sixteen. Winter dragged on for several weeks longer there than in New York, and it was a snowy year. We lived in a tiny white house beside a lake across which swept a fearsome wind and next to the shores of which my brother and I had to wait for our school bus. A brutal cold carved itself around our faces. No matter how many layers one draped over one's head, the cold penetrated one's brain mercilessly. If a scarf or glove came undone, our fingers were too frozen to reaffix it.

When the road was covered with heavy snow, we would watch from the picture window of the tiny house to see the yellow bus appear from around a curve and then dash down the long road to the bottom of the hill to the main road. There was always the possibility that we might arrive too late for the driver to see us. This meant hitchhiking, which kept us in the cold for an even longer time than waiting for the bus, since not much traffic came along these country roads. But even worse was the other possibility, namely, that the students already on the bus would see us, weighed down by book bags and lunches and winter gear, scramble along on the frozen road while the bus driver sat with a sour expression on her face and we prayed not to slip on the ice. I have always wondered that hell is depicted as a raging inferno; those chilling moments at the bus stop beside a frozen lake were among the most hellish I have ever known.

As an adult, I can appreciate the austere beauty and stoic mannerisms of this state's people. The fragrance of a cool pine forest in summer can be a transporting experience. But during that time, grief had closed my heart. The native New Hampshire drawl landed flat on my ears. Already stripped of words, I fell into silence.

For six months, starting with the car ride when we moved away from Newburgh, I barely spoke. Days would go by before I realized I had not uttered a word. As if sensing I could not be drawn into participation, in class teachers left me alone, with the exception of the more engaging Spanish teacher. The street language that had come so easily to my lips in Newburgh would have been, literally, out of place here. My accent sounded foreign. When I came from school, I usually went straight to my bedroom.

All that long winter and spring that melted so slowly into summer, I grieved. I mourned the absence of friends. I yearned for the sight of those green-shouldered mountains rising above a wide ribbon of river whose expanse flickered gray, blue, or silver. I missed the scorching black tar beneath my bare, calloused feet and I missed the cool meadow grass of the Bluff's precipice. My heart ached for the freedom and adventure of our river valley environs. Even the things I had disliked I missed for their sheer familiarity. While my mother's mixed feelings about the move subsided as she found a sewing spot by the picture window overlooking the lake and my father's energies were taken up by keeping up at work, I was the one who continued to resent leaving. Even my brother had accepted the move as a fresh start.

I took refuge in the Spanish teacher's classroom, assigning myself a glossary page of vocabulary words a day, just to kill time. I grasped at the remembered speech and volatile cadences of Marisol's family. If I closed my eyes in the overheated classroom, sleepy from waking up early to catch the bus, I could drowsily recall animated conversations in her family's basement kitchen. During the lonely lunch hour as I ate alone, I recalled the phrases Sandy shyly taught us in the walkers' group. Trying to hold on to the crux of cultures to which I no longer belonged, I obsessively arranged my hair in a million braids, as if I were still on the Heights, where we braided and rebraided each other's hair on porches overlooking the river. I listened to the 45 records trucked up here to the frozen North. The full, rich voices drenched with stored-up sunshine gave expression to my own experience of dispossession and longing. Playing my collection of 45 records over and over, I was trying to recapture the rhythms of my neighborhood. I was mourning the loss of soul.

There would be no going back. Although my circle of friends in high school would include teenagers of many backgrounds —

Puerto Rican, mixed European-American, Italian-American, Dominican, African-American, and Liberian — the intertwined knot
that had formed in me had unraveled. A white European-American
of dubious class background, I had been drawn into an intimate web
of culture and social overlap, not in an abstract way but through
specific interactions, through other people's lives melding into mine
in daily exchange. Being a child, I was susceptible to internalizing
this experience, like soft wax taking an imprint because it had not
yet cooled. Yet precisely because I am a white European-American
of dubious class background, when torn from the environment in
which this imprinting took place — these borderlands, this desert,
these crossroads — the fluid cultural categories closed. The wax
hardened.

Now I see that a loosening of the knot tangling together the
diverse cultural experiences would have inevitably happened over
time. My friends and I might have come from the same neighborhood, but society would have eventually dictated that we belong
to different worlds. High school would have disbanded our loyal-
ties and polarized our friendships. The riots that took place before
I was old enough to be conscious of them were a symptom of tensions that still governed the immediate world we were heading
into and to which we already belonged.

When it came down to the wire, my family left Newburgh because we *could*. Finding a new job, house, and community — and
having the educational background to be able to do so — was
made easier by the color of our skin and our ease with the English
language. Though my parents were reluctant to leave the house
we had loved, they also felt relieved that my brother and I would
get away. For me, however, being ripped away during the teenage
years was anything but liberating. It was the wrenching away that
turned my family's exodus into my exile.

Dispersion

I ran into Ruby's younger sister, Nicole, unexpectedly, when my
husband, Kenney, and I happened upon the health food restaurant

where she briefly worked, in the funky college town located directly north, but which might just as well be a million miles away. Several of the kids who had gone into the army — an easy way to escape this city — came back to take jobs in the ever-expanding sprawl and to live in the suburbs.

I ran into Luanne more recently in the library. She valiantly battles a heroin addiction while raising three daughters. Her husband still works on the apple farm. After the couple separated, she moved back to her mother's house — the same house where we visited her brother with the gunshot wound in the upstairs bedroom. She phoned me from there so that I could greet her family. One of her other brothers commented to me, bitterness in his voice, "Everybody else left, thinking they were getting out of the Burg, but they all came back eventually, anyway. I just saved myself the trouble of leaving."

I often run into Sandy at church. Her daughter, the student in my husband's catechism class, just had her own baby. Inconceivable it seems to me as I raise my own little brood, my childhood friend is now a grandmother. Our other grammar school friend, Karen, has two children and works in a supermarket outside town. From our class, Sandy has seen the two African-American sisters (whose father worked for IBM and who used to sit with the bus riders) in the bank. One of them is thriving, working a white-collar job and living in the town of Newburgh. The other, devastated after their father's death (they had already lost their mother as young children) became a drug addict and fell into prostitution. I look for her on the block two streets over, just on the other side of Broadway, where prostitutes walk up and down the street in front of the women's shelter. Is it selfish to be glad that I have not spotted her yet?

Of the white kids who used to drink beer and play cards at the dining room table of my parents' house, two have died, one of cirrhosis and the other of AIDS — probably infected through sharing needles during heroin use. Others have fared better: several who started off at West Point fixing refrigerators have learned a trade and moved out of the neighborhood. At the time of this writing, one of them had recently been elected mayor.

As JERUSALEM FELL to the Babylonians, a displacement related to but different from the Captivity occurred. In the deportations, the educated, the young, and the upper class were taken, chained, into exile. Other families, seeing that the ruined city held no future for them, left on their own. Making their way to surrounding Transjordan, Phoenicia, Syria, and Egypt, they lived alongside neighbors who perhaps did not understand their ways, but who might allow them to live in peace. Their departure neither voluntary nor coerced, they went into what would become known as the Dispersion.

When Cyrus of Persia came to power, displacing the Babylonians a full generation later, the Jews' Exile came to an end. Believing his strategy of allowing conquered peoples to return would be more effective than keeping them in captivity, he decreed that they were free to go home. The joy with which the exiles received the news can be easily imagined. After half a century in foreign lands, they could go back to the Promised Land to lead efforts of rebuilding Jerusalem.

Not as well recorded is the surprising evidence that in spite of Cyrus's magnanimous (and strategically calculated) decree, some did not return. Young people born in the Exile or Dispersion had never known the land for which their parents yearned; their tongues had grown used to the language of the empire. Young men accustomed to the more sophisticated Babylonian women were reluctant to marry unsophisticated native girls. Jerusalem, still in ruins, could hardly compete with the splendors of wealthy Babylonian cities. After glimpses of the riches of other lands, home no longer appeared as attractive. The link with the wondrous city of their parents' memories would not prove strong enough to lead them back.

Flight

Late in the spring of that year of exile, after much convincing, my mother allowed me to take a bus trip back to Newburgh. I had never traveled alone before, but I was determined to return to the river that flows both ways at the green cleavage of two mountains. At the end of a long day that began with a before-dawn departure and involved two changes of buses, I arrived back to my neighborhood. The air was sharp and sweet with early spring (it arrived earlier here than in New Hampshire), and the Bluff's vegetation was coming back to life after the dormancy of winter. Soaking in its familiar mountains and river, I felt numb with joy. Imagine, a whole week to spend!

My contentment at being home, however, was short-lived. The elderly ladies expressed relief that my brother and I had gotten out of Newburgh and wondered why I had come back at all. Marisol had started going out with a boyfriend I had never met. While glad to see me, her heart was elsewhere. It was during that week that her stepfather followed me into the bathroom. His objections to my keeping African-American friends and to my going out un-chaperoned caused tensions — or perhaps hid his guilt for trying to fondle my nightgown-clad body. I could not tell Marisol of my discomfort, and she could not defend me from her father. When he told me, through Marisol's translation, that I could no longer stay at their house, I sought refuge at Dolly's house.

The days passed too quickly, as if air had been rationed, as if the supply allowed one to breathe but not to fully expand one's chest. In a blurry scene that I can hardly reconstruct — so surreal did it seem at the time — one night I found myself with a man ten years my senior in the second story of an abandoned house. We had met casually in some forgotten circumstance and now became reacquainted. Like an obligatory pastime, courting was a sport that we all played in the neighborhood; sexual adventure was not only common, it was expected. Risk only made the boasting to take place later more interesting.

The man — known to me only by his street name, which I have long since forgotten — opened the door to the deserted house without forcing it, laughably mumbling some pretext of losing his key. We stumbled over torn-up floor boards and clambered up steps blocked by debris. Huddled in the damp chill of the unheated building, for the house was uninhabited, for the first time that trip I woke up. I awakened to the ridiculousness of my predicament.

Fortunately, as stupid as I had been to allow myself to get into that situation, the anonymous suitor did not try to take advantage of me. But something cold snapped inside me. As if something had seized me by the shoulders, trying to shake me to my senses. As if a rusted chain were being severed into multiple pieces. As if a cold, lapping tide had slapped my face with frigid salt water. I had to escape this madness called Newburgh.

The morning before I was to leave, as I got up from the bed I was sharing with Luanne in Dolly's house, I noticed that my money on the dresser had been disturbed. Counting it quickly, I found that at least twenty dollars was gone — money I would need to buy a return bus ticket. The same day, Luanne came home with a new, store-bought pair of shoes. I watched her face as I asked her about the money, and her expression confirmed what I already knew. This petty theft — which now seems understandable, and even inconsequential — was the wound that hurt the most. Adults couldn't be counted on and our kids' code of conduct might be skewed, but the loyalty that tied us together had been sacrosanct. It seemed as if Newburgh itself had betrayed me. The last link broke inside me, and I was free.

That night, the night before the bus was to carry me back to New Hampshire, I moved my things from Dolly's house. A friend of my mother's loaned me twenty dollars and allowed me to sleep on her couch. I spent my last night in Newburgh just up the street from Marisol's, whom I had to say good-bye to by phone, and next door to Angelique's, whose grandmother no longer allowed visitors. I could hardly wait for morning, for the escape that would take me away from here.

No longer could the memory of being beaten up on the sidewalk one summer afternoon make me cringe. No more would the bus riders in my school look down on us walkers. The green-shouldered mountains blankly shrugged at the sky, the same as usual. The river would flow — or glisten in sparkles, or roll in flat color, or undulate in lazy waves — this day, and every day, no matter what happened on its banks. The trains would charge past, their engine horns warning everyone in proximity to stay away. Let some other kids stand on the Bluff and wave to the *Clearwater* gliding past with full sails. Let some other girl stumble along these streets in search of friendship, or belonging, or love. Without the ability to wound, to betray, or even to bewilder me, Newburgh was like any other small depressed city in the Northeast. It would no longer be my home. My exile had turned into exodus. I turned my back on the past, and was gone.

Part Two

RETURN

** *Four* **

Viacrucis

It is almost noon on Good Friday in Newburgh during the year 2002, twenty years to the month since I left, betrayed. Our parish's English service just finishing, its worshipers stream out past the church facade. Already Spanish speakers are waiting to be let in. Hovering outside the building's huge wooden doors, they stand patiently on the stone steps, peering through rectangular windows to see if and when the church will make room for their coming. Once the building empties, they enter the church that has become their own.

As if a dam has been ruptured, the congregation floods the aisles. Those lucky enough to be assured a seat swiftly claim a pew. A steady flow of other arrivals inundates the church, and soon the wave swells in a crest that reaches the choir loft. Quickly, even there, the space becomes crammed. As on a crowded bus in the developing world, polite formalities are observed (*"discuple, con su permiso"*), although it would take a shoehorn to pry strangers and friends apart. Small children, who require — and receive — extra patience, get passed from lap to lap. Girls shimmer like miniature bridesmaids in ballooning dresses. Boys gleam with deliberately combed hair still wet or stiff with gel. Even those dressed more humbly appear meticulously arranged. Parish staff nervously remind parents in the choir loft not to allow their children near the edge of the balcony.

A somber, quiet mood prevails and is made more remarkable by the size of the gathering. Besides December 12 (the Feast of the Virgin of Guadalupe), Good Friday is the busiest day of the liturgical year in our Spanish-speaking parish community. Other holy days pack the church; indeed, by the end of every Sunday Mass there is standing room only in the back. But Good Friday and Guadalupe Day are something else. Just when one could not imagine a more densely packed crowd, additional latecomers are folded into the assembly. It is as if a bottomless chalice keeps on filling, as if a cup poured to the rim arches the convex surface of its liquid contents and yet does not spill. As if the lip of its rounded circumference embraces each drop and still makes room for more.

Our parish priest enters from the back of the church and the hush grows even deeper. Dressed in a simple white surplice, he himself, instead of an acolyte, carries the cross. A sea of people standing in the central aisle parts, allowing him to pass, then closes as a wake behind him. Three times he pauses to elevate the cross and to chant: *"Mirad el árbol de la cruz, donde estuvo clavado Cristo, el salvador del mundo."* ("Behold the tree of the cross on which was nailed Christ, the savior of the world.") Three times the response rises like a tide: *"Venid, adoremos."* ("Come, let us worship.") The intoxicating press of the crowd, the somber silence pierced only by very young children, the austere altar stripped of flowers or decoration, the plaintive voices of the choir for once deprived of guitars or percussion — all lead up to a singular, momentous expectancy. The Passion account is read and the mood settles into mourning. A people have come to take part in the suffering and death of Jesus Christ.

After the reading of the Passion, the priest and three liturgical ministers come forward with crucifixes for the veneration of the cross. The sea of people moves as a single wave toward the altar. This slow-moving, vast tide must trickle into four streams of faithful who will touch, kiss, and gaze upon the broken body on the crucifix. Normally during Mass, the communion line is efficient and quick-moving, since only a portion of those assembled receive communion. On Good Friday, however, everyone — squealing babies, tired-looking grandparents, stylishly dressed teenagers — no matter their age, no matter whether they have been to confession, no matter whether they are married in the church —

everyone approaches Christ. The sea of believers flows patiently, in increments. Emotion becomes palpable and almost overwhelming. Faces are drawn, grieving. The cantor's voice wails above our heads in a repetitive refrain. Sometimes tears that lay buried in the silt of silence are shed.

Everyone here has known suffering. Everyone here is in mourning. Perhaps it is for a child whose body lies far away, buried in the soil of one's home country. Or perhaps it is for one's mother or father who died alone in the *pueblo,* unseen one last time, because going home would have meant risking not being able to get back here to one's own family. Maybe the mourning is for the living. For the son or daughter immersed in gangs or lost to drugs. Or maybe it is vicarious mourning for others. For the neighbor swept away in the river while crossing the border or the cousin wandering the migrant trail, last seen three years ago. A residue of grief inundates the memory. It is a private moment, an intimate one. And yet this enormity of grief and loss is shouldered communally by a stream of innumerable people who somehow manage to make their way toward the cross without crushing each other.

When the flood of worshipers spills out into the streets, Christ's Passion is reenacted. In some countries and even in some parts of the United States, the Way of the Cross features actors in wigs and elaborate robes who play out the parts of the main characters in the narrative; this is a simpler affair. A huge wooden cross and a portable amplifier (strapped to the indefatigable don Felipe) are the only props. Children holding depictions of the Stations of the Cross display their pictures as the crowd pauses at designated resting places. Some recite the *Dios te salve* (Hail Mary) or join other straggling voices lifted in song, but often the crowd falls silent.

For seven years now my own little family has walked this Way of the Cross. We have been privileged to place our footsteps alongside those of this crowd. Becoming neighbors and fellow parishioners, we have gotten to know the sojourners on this walk. Earning a meager income at part-time jobs — in order to be freer for our children and for work in Catholic Worker style (and in my case, with the Grail women's movement) — and moving into Newburgh's notorious East End, we entered into the precariousness of this procession. Entering into shared relationships, we are allowed a glimpse into the rich inner life of people whom society considers poor. One year I was asked to read at one of the stations. Another year my husband was one of several men and women who shouldered the rough wood of the cross. But mostly, we just walk. If the day is warm, as it often is in the approaching spring, we will sweat with the exertion of the walk. If the day is chilly, exercise and the body heat of the crowd warm us considerably. There is one steep incline to be faced and two hills to walk down. The first leads to the city's main street, Broadway, and the second heads back toward our church overlooking the river.

This walk encapsulates the trials of the rest of the year, symbolizing many lifetimes' worth of crosses and suffering. I don't like to walk these streets, and so for me, it is a yearly penance, an annual sacrifice. We take the burdensome cross down the most drug-infested streets of this inner city. Roads are ragged with potholes, and one side street is so torn up it can no longer be considered paved. Walking by abandoned buildings and run-down rental apartments, we pass children playing on ripped-up porches while their parents hang out of windows with no screens. Some only pause to take in this sight to which they have become accustomed, but other onlookers sometimes jeer. Sometimes a heckler will call out, "I want to see your green cards." One year a kid urged his dog to lunge. The bilingual kids on the walk cringe, and a few men filter to the edges of the crowd, prepared to defend if necessary, but the procession continues on and nothing happens. The sight of a police escort deters more serious harassment. But as we pass the rows of run-down houses, sometimes other people, newer to the city, come out of their apartments. Making the sign of the cross over themselves, they stand in reverent silence or even join the walk for its duration.

This is an exodus journey. The recent immigrants in this Way of the Cross have escaped the poverty of their countries of origin to try their fortunes in the famed cities and farms of *el Norte*. Often the most adventuresome of their communities, they have set out on a pilgrimage fraught with danger in order to seek a better life for their children. Many of them are now literally reenacting the walk that brought them across the border. Others may have been born here, or had more advantages in immigrating, but all know that their exodus journey has not been easy. All of them are reclaiming the streets of a land that does not always welcome them as fully human.

This is also a journey into exile. The newly arrived may find here, not the Promised Land, but rather Babylon. Emigrating to a country whose minimum wage might be stretched to support two households, some have left a spouse and children behind. Working in order to send income back as well as to support themselves here, they hope to earn enough money to return home one day. Inevitably, it takes longer than hoped to set aside savings, or pay off medical bills incurred by a relative, or build a house bit by bit. Months stretch into years. The land of golden opportunity turns into a place of captivity. Every December and every Easter the disappointed who had planned to return can be heard to echo the Passover refrain, "Next year in Jerusalem."

Like Babylon, which benefited from the labor of Jewish exiles, this city profits from the displacement of indentured workers. Only the most sophisticated realize that the same policies of globalization that wrecked their local economies favor the very country to which they have come to work as vulnerable (and sometimes exploited) workers. But all recognize that the reality of *el Norte* is not as they had imagined. This procession takes us on the road of a crucifixion. The steps of our pilgrimage must be taken publicly because this is where their present-day Passion is carried out.

Christ's head is already crowned with thorns, bloodied by wire fences that separate families on two sides of the border. Jesus stumbles and falls at factories where immigrants toil for five dollars an hour in poorly lit, insufficiently ventilated buildings at jobs no one else will do. He meets the Women of Jerusalem at a guitar strings factory, where the Immigration and Naturalization Service

(I.N.S.) handcuffed some of the same women of this procession in a raid, taking them away in a windowless van to be deported.

Simon the Cyrene takes the cross at a storefront church where livelier services than ours will take place tonight, and a sorrowing Mary reaches out to her son at a Catholic church whose solemn property is used only once or twice a week. Jesus is stripped of his clothing in front of a *cantina* where men attempt to drink away their nostalgia or homesickness. His face is wiped by Veronica at the house of Alta Gracia, a brothel. His hands and feet are nailed to the cross on street corners where the young gamble with their own lives and those of others. Ever-present graffiti identifying which gang the street belongs to hover like an inscription above his head. As we arrive back to the church, Jesus' resurrection is foretold at the last station. At the parking lot across the street, in full view of the Hudson River, the good news is promised as waves sparkle in the sun on clear days — or brood gray and murky on overcast ones. The greening mountains rise watchful and silent in the background.

This Passion is not mine. There is a daily crucifixion that I witness, but that does not belong to me. My husband and I have chosen to move to this violent neighborhood replete with prostitution and drugs, but someday we will move our children (Rachel, Thomas, and Seamus) away from here. As citizens with legal status, as white people in a racist society, and as educated adults with college degrees, we exercise more choices at every fundamental social level. For the others on this journey there is no security of gaining a more promising future. The home we have chosen among the poor is simultaneously the unwanted captivity of exiles.

This is *not* our habitat — precisely for those reasons. Outsiders in a neighborhood that does not house others exactly like us, we share, anyway, in its benefits and inconveniences. On this walk, we taste what it means to be outsiders. Strangers to the language spoken here, we grope with faltering steps toward making ourselves understood or stumble to grasp the meaning being extended by another. Foreigners in our own church, we have learned what it is like to pray in a tongue not our own. Grafted onto a branch different from that of our upbringing (even though it grows on the same tree), it has taken years to arrive to the heart of its religiosity. This spirituality, this entering into the Way of the Cross, does not belong to us even though it has become a spiritual home.

And yet, this *is* the way of my Passion. These are the same streets I wandered as a child. As we walk the Stations of the Cross, we pass the sites that haunted my heart so many years. Here lived my best friend, Marisol, in her family's basement apartment, and here my neighbor Luanne's brother lay wounded upstairs, shuddering on a mattress with no sheets. The street with the most potholes is the one we walked to school each day, and these remaining factories used to be staffed by my friends' parents. This storefront church we pass is but a recent incarnation of the one I attended with Angelique and her grandmother, and the impressive (though deteriorating) Primera Asamblea temple we walk by is where I read words I could pronounce but not yet understand. In the neighborhood at the top of this same hill, I was beaten up one calm and unsuspecting afternoon. If we would continue up this street then turn to the left, the procession would arrive at my family's old house — the home we were forced to leave when my father lost his job.

These too are the streets of my exile. I have been away so long that I have literally become a stranger. During my first year back, I was standing outside church when Mayor Mickey, the retarded neighbor who occasionally used to baby-sit us, walked by. I was astounded when he did not recognize me.

The path of this Way of the Cross skirts the soup kitchen in the basement of the church gym. It is closed today, so I am spared the familiar dread of seeing the disheveled lineup of a different kind of procession. Predictable cycles of urban poverty take flesh in an anonymous litany: teenage pregnancy, low-paying jobs, welfare, light or heat or telephone cut off because of unpaid bills, slum rental apartments, drug and alcohol abuse, cheap cars that break down and broken homes that just keep getting more broken.

Most days, unable to stop myself, I search the line for the faces of childhood friends, all the while praying, "Please don't let them be here" — since that would mean they never made their own escape. If this parking lot outside the soup kitchen reunited me with childhood friends, what would I say to them? How could I bear to hear the stories of their failed lives, or worse, pretend that nothing *had* failed for them? How could I explain the fact that although I did come back to Newburgh, if I had never left I might be waiting in line with them? How could I explain my return?

Not only had *I* changed. I came back to find my hometown altered indelibly. These changes (not always met with approval by those who had stayed) were what brought me and my husband to Newburgh. Waves of middle-class flight had taken the more successful of my childhood friends away from this inner city, while jail, the army, or even early death had taken others. In returning, I discovered that the vacuum of jobs and housing created by their exodus had been filled by a new wave of exiles from many countries of origin.

Sojourns

Our parish includes believers from several Latin American countries, and every year we celebrate seven patronal feasts. I had wandered in Mexico and Central America as a seeker on my own exodus journey, something of a hybrid between a tourist and a pilgrim. I arrived back here to find the desert of this ruined city flowering with sojourners from those same lands. I came home to the South in the North.

In my own travels, I volunteered in Mexico for a year at a faith-based educational center. There I met a blond hitchhiker from California wearing a T-shirt that proclaimed Dorothy Day's memorable words, "The only solution is love." When Kenney stayed on to volunteer at the center, we fell in love in Cuernavaca, "the city of eternal spring," picturesque with its cobblestone streets and flowering terraces.

Kenney and I moved from the elegant center of this colonial city to stay, instead, in a much humbler *colonia,* whose paved road stops short of the neighborhood. Vistas of luscious gardens in enclosed courtyards gave way to views of kitchen gardens planted with medicinal herbs and flowers potted in used metal cans. From there, we visited the *pueblos* and *ranchitos* that are the original homes of families who had moved from the country to the mushrooming outskirts of cities. Those who remained still live off the land in isolated communities miles off paved highways. Since making a home in Newburgh we have made trips back and have met families who have relatives working here or on the farms just north. The home *I* left so I could explore their homelands has become the land of *their* discovery.

ON THIS PROCESSION, we pass the church school, a former elementary school that was closed decades ago. It now houses the parish's bilingual religious education program, where my husband and I have taught over one hundred Latino kids as catechists. We pass the telephone and wire services where the folks from the farms come each weekend to send money home; my husband knows many of them by name through his job at a migrant health clinic. We pass ethnic grocery stores and restaurants where men separated from their families buy their lonely foodstuff or indulge in a real meal. We pass the homes of friends and *compadres* (parents of our godchildren) who have shared with us the joys and struggles of their daily life over these seven years.

Here, in Newburgh, for just this particular moment in time, our steps have traced this people's Way of the Cross. I have walked the ruined streets of my childhood with a suffering people who refuse to be broken. Who are here to meld their Passion stories to that of Jesus Christ's. Who have come to this place to set their story of exile within the larger story of salvation — an exodus story. And I have sought my own redemption not *within* but *beside* theirs, in a shared procession toward the river sparkling in the sun.

This is an exodus march, a journey through the wilderness. The Hebrew people coming out of slavery had to pass this way, their steps in the desert circling in on themselves until they finally allowed themselves to fall into the gravity of their own freedom. They might be distracted by the golden calf of consumerism, or trivialize their many blessings by falling into *envidia* (envy) or *chisme* (gossip). They would definitely get to know intimately their own hunger and thirst, and suffer the extremes of bitter cold by night and scorching sun by day in the relentless desert. Divisions over leadership might arise, and questions about authority. But it was on the exodus journey that God established a covenant with God's people.

WITH ROOTS STRETCHING BACK before written history, the exodus story celebrates spring's arrival. The earth's yearly renewal found a powerful expression in the unblemished purity of newborn lambs. Grafted to the ancient narrative of a people who sojourned through the desert in search of freedom, many layers of symbolism combine into one liturgical practice. Diaspora only strengthens the desire of a people who long for home. The Exodus must be reenacted — even in the midst of deprivation, complaints, lapses into idolatry, and power struggles. Each year this story of slavery and liberation must be retold by the Jewish people, not simply *repeated* but actually *relived* in the remembering.

For Christians, the Paschal Mystery comes to us through this living memory. In the culmination of his ministry, at the Passover meal, Jesus identified himself in the context of the exodus story. His Journey to Jerusalem ended with this liturgical practice; the meaning of his life was made not only visible but even palpable at that table. Christ, the unblemished lamb, is offered as the ultimate sacrifice in order to end all propitiatory sacrifice. Exercising complete freedom, he chose to be emptied of all that he possessed — even his life — so that others might find the way to liberation.

Jesus' words over the Passover meal, uttered just before the final moments of his own exodus journey, ask us not to mimic a formula but to take on his very voice. His Passion does not ask us to simply duplicate his actions, but to model our own lives on his, melding them into the single Paschal Mystery carried out endlessly over time. As on manna in the desert, we will be fed a never-ending Eucharist *if we willingly take on our own exodus journey.* Wherever we find ourselves, at whatever resting place in the desert, a table will be set overflowing with abundance. In the final telling, although it speaks of leavings and wanderings, the exodus story is about coming home.

These seven years have been a journey of return. Coming back, I have enjoyed moments of a strange, contemplative peace as I write while looking out my window over the soup kitchen. I arrived only to embark on an invisible, internal journey. I found an inexplicable homecoming in the Way of the Cross that wanders a torturous path through the streets I had escaped. Christ calls us to walk the exodus journey, even when it takes us to Calvary. How could one not be filled with gratitude, being shown the face of the Beloved by being taken to the foot of the cross?

Spanish will never flow to my tongue fluidly, like English. I will never live in my own experience what it is to illegally cross a border — or worse, to live in daily anxiety as an undocumented immigrant. Racism will never curtail my life's possibilities. I will always be an outsider to this procession incarnating a people's Passion, and yet, and yet . . . its steps echo in my blood. Somehow this people's exodus story has awakened my own.

As we walked this journey, strangers became friends. As I welcomed the recently arrived, I found that in tracing their footprints or surrendering my tongue to their idiom's poetry, I became the guest at a feast more abundant than I could have imagined. Accompanying a people of faith who allowed me to place my footsteps beside theirs, I found myself converted. I had to become a newcomer to the city of my childhood, welcomed, nourished, and taught by foreigners, in order to come home to a Passover feast at which we are "no longer strangers and aliens, but . . . citizens with all the saints and also members of the household of God" (Ephesians 2:19).

Homecoming

> *Glorious things are spoken of you,*
> *O city of God....*
>
> *And of Zion it shall be said,*
> *"This one and that one were born in it";*
> *for the Most High will establish it.*
> *The Lord records, as God registers the peoples,*
> *"This one was born there."*
>
> — *Psalm 87*

While Sandy was the first person from my past I actually talked to, Karen's mother was the first person I recognized. On Sundays since we began attending Spanish Mass, we used to drive up Broadway to the Italian bakery, which has been in operation since I was a child. (To my and my brother's chagrin, my parents found it too expensive to frequent — we went there only rarely.) It was with some satisfaction that I began to take my husband and our daughter to this bakery, one of the few remaining businesses left downtown. It became a ritual for us to enjoy a *cappuccino* and biscotti for the baby while looking out over the busy main street.

One Sunday a figure caught my eye. A female form wrapped in an ungainly layering of garments meandered across the wide expanse of Broadway. Pushing an old-fashioned wire shopping cart, she paused often to maneuver its rickety wheels. Stopping at the garbage barrels, she went through their contents, collecting cans. The sight is not an unusual one in Newburgh, but something seemed vaguely familiar about this woman's thin frame and hesitant way of moving her hands. From my vantage point in the bakery window, I could see her gnarled, knobby fingers and fragile wrists. A patterned scarf tied under her chin covered all but a tuft of hair which spilled out over her forehead. When she turned around, I was able to look her full in the face: blue eyes watchful but strangely vacant, garishly dyed hair, fire-engine-red lipstick. Suddenly I was transported back in time. I recognized her then and recalled one visit to an apartment on this same block.

The living room, though shabby, had many windows, which let in streams of afternoon light. Karen and I, still in our school uniforms, deliberated what to make for dinner while her brother watched television. Their mother was just coming home from her shift at a factory job. She arrived to find that her oldest son, sulking on the couch, had skipped high school *again*. Turning from a brewing argument that he seemed to invite, she turned to the mirror to paint her face. We girls watched, fascinated by a glimpse into this grown-up ritual that Karen's mother practiced for each man in a long string of boyfriends.

From the bakery window, I wondered if lipstick had become an unbreakable habit or whether Karen's mother still found someone to date. I wondered what ever happened to her son, the lanky blond teenager who refused to go to school. I wondered how Karen handles her mother's sorry state. These days, I often catch sight of Karen's mother wandering up and down Broadway, sorting trash or stopping into a shop for a cup of coffee. Her waif-like figure flits like a ghost from the past while her haggard face bears the simplicity of a child — fire-engine-red lipstick notwithstanding. Like Mayor Mickey, Karen's mother does not talk to me. Judging from her absent manner, I doubt she would recognize me even if we spoke.

It is exactly twenty years to the month since that tearful ride away from Newburgh — an exile that turned into a willing exodus. When my family left here, having lost our house and driven by necessity to abandon our beloved river, I had cried the whole ride to New Hampshire. But after a disastrous return, I left again — this time with a grateful heart. Repeating the same trek north to rejoin my family in New Hampshire, I watched winter melting all along the countryside from the windows of a Greyhound bus. I had escaped. My ruined generation had remained. When I come across those who, like me, left and returned, or when I run into the few who stayed to battle Newburgh's demons and emerged victorious (like the city's current mayor — one of the young men who used to play cards at our dining room table — who overcame a heroin addiction to work as a drug rehabilitation counselor), we greet each other in shared, common amazement: we are survivors. A remnant.

AT THE BIRTH of our first child, Kenney and I had moved to the Catholic Worker farm, now located just north of Newburgh, where my parents live. For my husband, returning to the Catholic Worker meant continuing a way of life that began for him during high school in the Los Angeles Catholic Worker community. For me, the move brought us closer to a program and retreat center run by the international women's movement to which I belong — and, of course, nearer to my parents (our daughter's doting grandparents). While at the Catholic Worker farm, my husband started doing outreach to the nearby migrant farmworker camps. As was our custom since we met in Mexico, we looked for a Spanish Mass, and found one — in Newburgh.

After two years at the farm, and having had a second child, we wanted to find a place of our own. Being committed to full-time parenting (divided between us), we knew our income would be quite limited. We had not planned to move to Newburgh. But after realizing that housing in the surrounding towns was beyond our means, we asked the Sisters in our parish if they knew of a cheap apartment. Just as we had given up hope of finding anything we could actually afford, one Sunday after Mass they approached us. Would we be interested in renting an apartment next door to them? The owner was willing to rent it at low cost to someone who would take responsibility for the building.

As the owner was away working on another property (a farm he had bought farther north), we had to take our first look over the fence from the Sisters' backyard. A grape arbor some sixty years mature shaded a patio outside the kitchen door. Steps led to an overgrown upper garden with red currant bushes proliferating at the foot of the stairs. Raspberry bushes grew in a frenzy. Fruit trees crowded each other for space while vegetables competed with weeds for room. The owner had bought the two back lots for $200 apiece from the city and left its trees to grow tall and leafy. From the lower garden, a rooster crowed full-throated and defiant, and hens clucked in the cool of its shaded woods. We were enchanted.

The thrill faded and was almost — but not quite — extinguished once we entered the house. The building smelled of mold and must. Its odors probably wafted through the creaks in the floorboards from the first story, where the owner operated a used (*very* used) book store. Occupied and added-onto in sections for some 150 years, during the white flight of the 1970s the building had been abandoned. When the owner bought the house for a couple of thousand dollars, it was in a sorry state of disrepair. Though he had done his best to fix it up over the years, its previous neglect was still very much in evidence.

Worded simply, the house was a mess. Rows and rows of precariously balanced glass jars were stacked everywhere, hundreds or thousands of them: the owner, who grew up on a farm, thought they might come in handy someday for canning. The linoleum and the interior paint had not been redone in decades, and the kitchen appliances had long ago crusted over. Every window pane was filthy, streaked with grime both inside and outside. Most arresting of all, during the spring he had brought a dozen just-hatched chicks inside to keep them safe and warm — and never moved them out. Now half-grown, they roamed the apartment, roosting in the bedroom.

But the huge front room (probably at one time two rooms that were joined by knocking down the wall separating them) opened into a welcoming space with three tall windows and walls painted four different, vivid colors. The spacious garden eased our homesickness for the fifty acres of green farmland we had just left, and the patio would make an ideal play area for the children. Best of all, the house stood across from the parish church and next door to a very dependable set of neighbors, the Sisters.

Preparing the house to make it habitable, I was slowly getting used to the idea that although I had never planned to, I was returning to Newburgh. Moving back with a family of my own, I could hardly believe that the same skinny corn-braided girl with black-soled bare feet who had played on the Bluff would bring her own children here.

The first night we were to sleep in our new home was the loneliest of my life, although I was not alone. On that particular evening in late August, Kenney and I were exhausted from a day spent cleaning out the apartment to make it inhabitable. The chickens moved out, we scrubbed down the bedroom. We were racing to prepare the house for our first night in Newburgh. But first, we had arranged to bring the parish priest to say Mass at an apple farm. Taking a respite from cleaning, we drove out to the farm with baby Thomas and toddler Rachel in the back seat and the priest following behind in his car. After Mass, the crew leader brought out soda and chips while our children played with those of the crew.

On that clear August evening, a chill in the air spoke of autumn's coming. The moon, luminous and bright, rose over the hills, slowly untangling itself from the gnarled arms of apple trees along the ridge as it ascended. Smoke from some neighbor's woodstove drifted into the brash air descending from a wide-open sky. Standing about in the drab dining room overly lit by fluorescent bulbs and later enveloped in pleasant darkness outside on the grass, we enjoyed amiable conversations with our *compadres* (we had become godparents for their children). Only after getting the kids into the car and heading "home" did the sense of strangeness hit.

We had to pass the driveway of the Catholic Worker farm, where my parents (and now, also my brother) live, where we had lived for the past two years. But instead of making the habitual left turn slowly onto the unpaved road that crosses a creek and curves up a hill, we kept going. The moment we passed the dirt driveway, our half-asleep daughter turned her tousled head to see why we had "missed" the turn. Instead of embracing an even deeper quiet than the stillness we had just come from at the apple farm, we headed into the raucous fray of a summer's Saturday night in Newburgh. As if approaching a foreign land, we drove toward the lights of the city with its vaguely threatening streets. I felt a sudden, sharp pang. We were going "home," but it did not feel like home. Why had we left the comforting hospitality of the country to reside in this decadent city?

Worse than being unfamiliar, the city to me at night was all too familiar. It held the ghosts of a past I would rather forget. Images flashed through my mind: night falling as Ruby and I crept out of the housing projects, surreptitiously crossing town to the safety of our own neighborhood . . . a barefoot, wild-haired bunch of kids racing, enthralled, on the Bluff at dusk . . . walking home from Angelique's storefront church after choir practice, or bundling with Marisol's family into her half-sister's station wagon. I had left it all behind. I had made my exodus. I had moved on from here, and I was glad of it. But here I was, coming back — with my husband and two children — to my old neighborhood, inconceivably, to our new home. Instead of the relief of familiarity, I felt a hollow, aching sense of *soledad* (loneliness).

That night we were kept awake by roving bands of youth. Their boom boxes and conversations — whether jovial or confrontational — sounded too loud to our ears, accustomed as they were to the country's quiet. Tossing and turning on our mattresses laid out on the wood floor, I kept asking myself, "What am I doing here?" but could find no satisfactory answer. Whatever politically correct or even radically pious answers came to mind didn't assuage my fears and doubts in the middle of the night.

Newburgh is the place you are supposed to leave once you "make it." Those who want to make a contribution usually come back in professional roles, as social workers or others in the helping professions. Living in the towns and commuting to the inner city allows them to preserve their own sanity. More religious-oriented types who do immerse themselves in the community, like Sisters or Catholic Workers, are usually not from the poverty-stricken places where they serve and so can more easily cultivate the healthy sense of detachment that eluded me in that moment. I was not on mission. This was a city that had once been my home but that, thankfully, had ceased to be. I felt no sense of gratitude in returning here, only a bewildered wonder at life's ironies and, it must be admitted, a slight sense of defeat.

My girl friends and I used to brag that if we ever came back, we would do so "wearing panty hose," meaning as somebody important. The jarring discrepancy of returning here with a husband and children who had no connection whatsoever with this city of my childhood struck a dissonant chord. After a sleepless night, we got up to continue the drudgery of scrubbing, sanding, and painting the apartment. Sorting through the chaff of the past to establish a foothold in the present. Trying to open my heart to this city, this neighborhood, this house that I would share with Kenney and our children. Making it home.

> *Do not remember the former things,*
>   *or consider the things of old.*
> *I am about to do a new thing;*
>   *now it springs forth, do you not perceive it?*
> *I will make a way in the wilderness*
>   *and rivers in the desert.*
>   *— Isaiah 43*

In my heart, a voiceless message clearer than spoken words echoed reassuringly. "Don't be afraid," Christ whispered to me. "I will be your home."

** *Five* **

Explorers

Let this be recorded for a generation to come,
*   so that a people yet unborn may praise the Lord;*
that when God looked down from the holy heights,
*   from heaven the Lord looked at the earth,*
to hear the groans of the prisoners,
*   to set free those who were doomed to die;*
so that the name of the Lord may be declared in Zion,
*   and God's praise in Jerusalem,*
when peoples gather together,
*   and kingdoms, to worship the Lord.*

— Psalm 102

As if by delving into the city's past I hoped to understand my own, in this return I greedily took in the details of its origins. Reconstructing the external markers that point to Newburgh's deeper reality, I was groping for a landing for my own feet. Without a temporal and spatial framework with which to understand the timeline and the geography that cradle my own, I wandered, lost, in my own home city.

If I could just understand the background that gave shape to its identity, I thought, maybe I could understand my place in it. Exploring the slippery landscape of the sheer drop of the face of Storm King Mountain or tracing the castle exploded into ruins on Bannerman's Island, it was my own inner geography that I longed to chart. But as I peeled apart the past's decades, centuries, millennia, I felt its grip on my own memories loosen. My intuition told me that this was the only way I could free myself of Newburgh's hold on me. To reach the city's psyche, I had to understand its history.

ON CLEAR MORNINGS in summer after a previous day's rain, the mountains appear as cutouts against the sky. Their deep green velvet ridges stand in sharp contrast to a vivid blue background. In winter, snow lines the ridges. Rows of trees rise, brown and stiff as a crew cut. On hazy mornings, a layer of mist lightly veils the edges of the mountains' shoulders, their topography revealed in undulating curves. If it is cloudy, a curtain of fog shrouds the change of medium from land to water. As if sky suddenly melted into water, not even the foot of the mountains can be seen. If it is *really* cloudy, the river itself disappears. Bannerman's Island fades into oblivion. Even Storm King Mountain, the ancient granite formation once esteemed by Native Americans as a sacred site, and West Point, the imposing fortress that hones an empire's top military leaders, are hidden from view. Somewhere along here two centuries ago, the king of sea robbers, Captain Kidd, buried a million dollars' worth of stolen treasures. This particular bend in the river discloses and reveals. Its history alternately allures and repels.

In 1524, the Italian explorer Giovanni da Verrazano saw the Hudson River, from where he landed at the open mouth of the Atlantic, but he did not explore the river's course. The Portuguese explorer Estevan Gomez may have traveled partway up the river around 1525. Unknown traders, probably French and Dutch, reached as far as Albany during this same period, though the exact year of their expedition, like their identities, is unknown. English explorer John Cabot may have found his way here (his nautical records suggest the possibility, but evidence is inconclusive). Some historians even believe that a Viking ship led by Thorfin Karlsefni arrived here from Straumfjord as far back as the year 1003.

Henry Hudson and his crew on the *Half Moon* made the journey from the site of modern-day Manhattan to what is now Peekskill in half a day of clear sailing weather. Believing that a channel existed between the Pacific and Atlantic Oceans, they thought they had found it: after navigating Breakneck's treacherous turn, they emerged into this breathtaking open valley. At the location that is now Newburgh, they discovered that the river water carries a strong saline content. Not realizing that they had underestimated the strength of oceanic undercurrents (conversely, freshwater streams from the Hudson can be detected one hundred miles into the open Atlantic), they assumed they had found the fictitious channel.

But Henry Hudson's two voyages must be remembered for another error in judgment. Although the exact spot remains unknown, somewhere around this area the explorer decided to make contact with the first peoples of this land. An initial encounter had gone well when native representatives came out to greet him with gifts. When Hudson and a few of his sailors went ashore to reciprocate, it did not take long for things to go awry.

I imagine that Newburgh might have been the site of this occasion almost four hundred years ago. Is this where Henry Hudson disembarked from the *Half Moon*, leaving his ship anchored at bay? Is this where the anxious crew kept watch in uncertainty for their captain's return? Where Native Americans expertly skimmed the waves in long, slim canoes to approach the foreign ship? Foreigners and natives could not communicate except through signs. As the longboat came closer, the sailors on board panicked. A skirmish ensued, and the Native Americans on the longboat were attacked. One was shot. When Hudson returned from his visit (which had gone cordially), he found the delicate opening note of peace already ruptured by dissonance. Taking two hostages to ensure their own safety, the crew hastily lifted anchor and sailed north.

History does not tell us if the two hostages were ever released, or even who the men on the longboat were. They may have been members of the same settlement as the one Hudson was even then visiting, or they might have been delegates sent by another tribe (not one but many Native American groupings populated these banks). Were they motivated by curiosity? diplomatic protocol? greed and the desire to trade?

Arriving at Albany, when it became clear that the fabled channel did not exist — or at least not along these waterways — Hudson's ship turned around and headed back toward the Atlantic. The second trip would not end as providentially. If Henry Hudson had gone back, his crew might not have later mutinied, setting Hudson, his son, and eight others adrift in the frigid Hudson Bay. If the *Half Moon* had not been locked in by ice all winter, several sailors would not have died of starvation and others might not have attacked an Eskimo village for food in their desperation. If one of the survivors had not broken their oath of secrecy, the story might have gone unrecorded. The remaining sailors finally made it back to Europe, where they tried to settle into normal civilian lives. Unable to find peace with so many deaths on his conscience, one of the mutinous sailors confessed. His fellow survivors died in dungeons.

Natives

The valley's first settlers, of course, were the native peoples with whom Hudson's crew clashed in that early encounter. When the river banks were bulldozed for the Newburgh-Beacon bridge, artifacts such as arrowheads and cooking instruments thousands of years old were unearthed. Scholars vary widely on approximating the original size of the Native American population. At the time of Henry Hudson's arrival, somewhere between thirty-five and one hundred thousand Native Americans inhabited in the Hudson River Valley. Living mainly near freshwater sources, they fished and harvested plentiful oyster beds. In spring and summer, they collected a variety of wild berries and fished with nets for their staple striped bass, perch, and shad. They fished for rarer varieties as well, such as oyster toad fish brought north from tropical waters by the Gulf Stream. Some tribes were ambitious enough to hunt whales, porpoises, and seals. In fall, they harvested corn, squash, and beans. During the fall and winter months, the tribes moved farther inland for protection from the wind and cold, surviving by hunting. Deer were caught by being chased into the river, where hunters waiting in canoes shot or clubbed them as game.

Feuds between tribes might have bitter consequences: rivalries sometimes erupted into raids on neighboring settlements. Each warrior was to practice a death song, which he should chant as long as possible while being tortured to death by captors. Since the ordeal might last two or three days, carried out by the entire enemy clan (beginning with the children, who branded burning coals onto the captive's chest), such a feat would have required extraordinary strength and courage. Being captured did not equal defeat; giving up one's death song was what meant one had been beaten. Victory consisted in persisting to chant until the exact moment of death, meaning that though one's body had expired, one's spirit had never been conquered.

Within fifty years, skirmishes with Europeans, migration to more remote areas, smallpox, and measles wiped out an estimated 90 percent of the native population. Some Native Americans were forced into slavery; others into indentured servanthood. In a playing out of that initial encounter between longboats and the *Half Moon*, Europeans displaced the First Peoples from the banks of the river.

Settlers

> *God turns a desert into pools of water,*
> *a parched land into springs of water.*
> *And there God lets the hungry live,*
> *and they establish a town to live in;*
> *they sow fields, and plant vineyards,*
> *and get a fruitful yield.*
> — *Psalm 107*

In 1620, the Pilgrims requested permission to establish their settlement on the banks of the Hudson but were turned down and instead set their sights on the Massachusetts coast. German settlers, convinced by its descriptions that the Hudson River Valley was the new Rhineland, came here fleeing persecution. In 1709, a group of fifty-three German Palatines (twenty-four of them children) arrived to found the first European settlement at this site. Germans in the village were soon outnumbered by Scotch English, who came to the area beginning in 1743. A number of Dutch settlers also made their way here; thanks to their descendants, the Dutch Reformed church would be built. In 1752, the settlement was officially christened: "Newburgh."

The home of a whaling fleet until overfishing caused the whale population's decline, the settlement expanded as the area around it exploded with the growth. By 1776, the population of Newburgh had grown to about six hundred inhabitants. During the Revolutionary War, George and Martha Washington's Headquarters (which I can see from my window as I write — the site of my first-grade class trip and the nearest wide-open space where our children play) served as the cornerstone in a network of barracks, mills, munitions shops, and farms. A ferry at the Newburgh landing transported in turns the some eight thousand soldiers stationed nearby. The headquarters was the site at which the revolutionaries masterminded a surprising invention: in an ingenious strategy, the army strung a huge metal chain across this bend of the Hudson River to deter British ships from being able to enter the valley.

After the war, Newburgh's strategic location changed from a military to a commercial one. The river waterway allowed shipping of agricultural and manufactured products to the burgeoning New York City. The invention of the steamship in 1807 — launched from this very waterfront — heightened Newburgh's commercial advantage. Broadway, I learned, had been intentionally made as a wide avenue in order to accommodate cattle and wagonloads of agricultural produce being driven in from the surrounding countryside toward the docks. The completion of the Erie Canal in 1825 (dug by free African-Americans and by Irish and German immigrants for fifty cents a day) allowed trade with interior parts of the country.

Locally, new farms and factories sprang up at a rapid pace. In 1800, Newburgh was a village; by 1865, it had become a city. From its earliest days, the city served as a port of entry for newcomers seeking work in the land of opportunity. Railroad construction and the shipping docks brought transient laborers, while other newcomers more inclined to stay settled on farms. Farming hit its peak quickly, in the mid-nineteenth century. The first blow to agriculture came when the valley's grain mills were driven out of business by cheaper prices for grain from the western frontier.

On the heels of the steamboat era, railroads ushered in a new transportation age. By the third quarter of the nineteenth century, both sides of the Hudson River Valley were lined with tracks used by competing railroad companies. Through stock market manipulations, the well-known capitalist family the Vanderbilts drove Harlem Railroad stock down — then bought it. The freight trains of my childhood that used to flatten coins we laid carefully on the gleaming silver tracks are the successors to this buyout. To this day, passenger trains are restricted to the east side of the river while freight trains remain relegated to the west side. (Occasionally there is talk of opening the west side for passenger traffic, with no results.)

Soon the area led the country in the production of candles, soap, dairy products, pianos, felt, handbags, paper products, rugs, carriages, and clothing — notably, felt hats, which were all the rage. At one point, Newburgh became famous for its manufacture of lawn mowers; at another, for a brief span a Newburgh company pioneered an unheard-of development in communications technology — the telephone. The immediate environs boasted the biggest brickyards of the late nineteenth century, providing a major source of jobs until woolen mills replaced them as the area's largest employers. By 1890, the city's population had exploded to some twenty-three thousand inhabitants drawn by the prospect of work.

But the river and land suffered from such sudden expansion. The grain mills had not only gone out of business due to competing prices from the West, but also because soil depletion had lowered the yield and quality of crops. And by 1872, the Hudson River was already so polluted that Poughkeepsie residents refused to drink its water even though it had been processed in a newfangled invention, a water treatment plant.

The river had been overfished. The shad population (an important food source for larger fish) crashed in the early 1800s. The sturgeon so admired by the sailors on the *Half Moon* (called a "living fossil" since its makeup has been virtually unchanged since prehistoric times), was overfished by 1880 and almost extinct by 1920. Since the sturgeon returns annually to fresh water to spawn, its yearly sojourn made it easy prey. The one to three million eggs held in the female sturgeon's abdomen were especially prized by sophisticated New Yorkers with a taste for caviar.

Borders

In my research into the city's archives, I learned that immigrants to Newburgh at the turn of the century had been scapegoated for the city's problems long before the immigrants my husband and I know — or even the migrants such as Dolly and Garrett my family had known — ever came north. While Newburgh's industry *required* unskilled, cheap labor (by 1909, the city held 104 factories manufacturing products worth $10 million a year), its residents blamed the poverty of the working poor on ... well, the poor.

The sudden growth of industry and agriculture, with its concomitant population surge, relied on a fluctuating and sometimes volatile system of commerce. Businesses moved in and out. Factories started up and closed down. Unemployment due to job injuries or layoffs became common. Availing themselves of immigrants' cheap labor, leaders neither in government nor business developed the infrastructure to support them.

Often a business's success depended on factors beyond local control. For example, tourism became a mainstay of the local economy just south of Newburgh in the late 1800s. Epidemics in New York City made the Hudson Valley attractive, and vacationers flocked to resort hotels built along the river. During holidays and summer months, the hotels filled to capacity. But when improved transportation could take tourists farther north up the river, the resort business suddenly collapsed in just three seasons (the summers of 1881, 1882, and 1883).

Angrily looking for a scapegoat, disappointed investors belatedly blamed the collapse on "the payday riot" of 1883, when immigrant railroad workers brought in to expand train lines broke into a brawl. Militia were called to restore the peace. The riot may have begun when resentful workers found themselves shortchanged for a week of backbreaking work. Or, as critics claimed, it may have been triggered by the alcohol consumption that began every week on payday. Whichever is true — or perhaps a bit of both — anti-immigrant sentiment was on the rise.

A record of Newburgh's demographics at the turn of the century revealed less than a quarter of the population to be U.S.-born. Immigrant and migrant groups included workers of "Italian, Irish, Negro [sic], English, Slavish, German, Polish, Scotch, Hebrew [sic], Austrian, Syrian and Norwegian" backgrounds who had flocked to take jobs in the area. Newspapers routinely engaged in what would today be called "racial profiling." Emphasizing the brutality of crimes allegedly committed by immigrant suspects, such coverage inflamed the anti-immigrant fervor that was already ignited.

A report on social problems (already in 1912 Newburgh was known as a "problem" city) noted that Newburgh was known throughout the valley as a "typhoid town." Defective sanitation, polluted water, and a contaminated milk supply combined with poor living conditions enabled the rapid spread of disease. A survey of the East End estimated that 10 percent of the population lived as borders in lodging houses set up to accommodate single men and women who had recently arrived to the city in search of work. (Women made up a third of the unskilled workers.) That 95 percent of the homes in this part of the city had no bathtubs tells not only of poor hygiene but also of housing that had to "make do" for an influx of newcomers.

Workers in skilled trades, which were organized, actually earned decent wages. But unskilled laborers brought home poor earnings. Women made under six dollars a week for a fifty-four-hour work week, and children made even less. Almost a thousand children of school age did not attend school at all, but joined their family members working in factories. The report from the turn of the century estimated that there was a saloon for every seventy-seven men. Alcoholism led to family disintegration. The cycle repeated itself as young people from broken homes became more likely to fall into vices. In the 1920s and 1930s, Newburgh became known throughout the valley as a center of gambling and brothels.

A historical perspective helped me to understand that the city's contemporary reputation resembles the one it acquired around the turn of the century. The story of the prostitutes who now wander the streets near the women's shelter, with its spilled-out bags of clothes and bread, began with a preface long before their own personal tragedies occurred. The drug dealers who cluster on our corner, wearing gold chains and brand-new sneakers and sporting cell phones, have inherited a sinister entrepreneurial streak passed on through generations of forebears. It also helped me to understand that the city's lifeblood pulses in its people, sojourners who have made it this far on their own exodus journeys.

Deportations

> O Lord, God of my salvation,
>   when, at night, I cry out in your presence,
> let my prayer come before you;
>   incline your ear to my cry.
>
> — *Psalm 88*

My first awakening to the plight of undocumented workers came during a catechism class. From the Sisters in our parish, I heard that the I.N.S. had raided two cookie factories in New Jersey that employed some two hundred workers from Newburgh — most of them undocumented. In class that night, one of my students seemed withdrawn. When I asked her what was the matter, she told me her father had been deported. While they had heard from him and knew that he was all right, they did not know when he would rejoin the family, since returning would mean making the perilous trip back across the border. Her mother worried about the rent money now that the household's main wage earner was gone. In addition, they would now have to accumulate savings to pay for his return.

On four consecutive Thursdays during Lent one year, different factories in Newburgh were raided. One friend of ours, don Enrique, was working in a light fixtures factory when *la Migra* came (that is, the I.N.S., the Immigration and Naturalization Service). He quickly hid inside a large cardboard box and went uncaught. Others were not so lucky. Workers found without papers were stuffed into vans to be taken to detention centers, their wrists handcuffed. Since some factories in Newburgh hire more women than men, mothers who should have been picking up their children at the bus stop after school found themselves in detention instead. Some complained that they had received neither the right neither to legal counsel nor to a phone call. Only relatives who themselves had legitimate identification of legal status might visit or sign out detainees on bail.

The consequences of the first raids were drastic, with immediate deportations. Like my student's father, many people were dumped across the border that same day. Subsequent raids, though not as dramatic, proved to be just as burdensome. Purchasing a one-way plane ticket to demonstrate at an appointed court date, one could "buy" extra time and thus work a few months longer or put one's business in order before leaving the country. Equally important, one would recover the *fianza* (down payment for bail money) that relatives and friends had chipped in. Presenting one's self to the appropriate government authority in one's home country, one could obtain the letter the I.N.S. requires to redeem the *fianza*.

NEWBURGH SERVES AS A PORT of entry for every incoming migrant or immigrant group in the valley. Newburgh is everyone's port of entry but no one's lasting inheritance. The city launches each ethnic group, propelling the best and brightest onto an exodus trail leading out of here, yet remains behind bereft, a forsaken harbor, merely one more stop along the exodus journey. A desert oasis, here immigrants pitch their tents, but their children will leave once they realize this is not the Promised Land of milk and honey they long for.

When I was growing up here, Newburgh's population had dwindled to the lowest point in its history since the boom of the 1800s. And now, inconceivably, I have brought my own little family to add to its numbers. I wonder whether we too will one day shake the dust from our feet and leave, no sentiment wasted, no tears shed. One lives in "the Burg" just for now, *mientras* (meanwhile), until somewhere better can be found. It is a wasteland, a crack city. A Babylon, a Promised Land turned sour, a desert that must be wandered before one finally comes home. A typhoid town and a prostitute's haven. Drug dealers' territory and turf of minimum-wage factories. A crossroads, a no-man's land, and an in-between place. A border.

Moises

Six-week-old Moises had not yet had his first bath. His mother, Carmen, asked, with all the shyness of her native Guatemalan village, would I show her how to bathe him? Setting out the baby tub we conferred about water temperature, adding cold then hot until it felt just right. Moises fussed as we gently unpeeled the many layers of clothes protecting him from *aire* (drafts). As I gently lowered him into the lukewarm bath, his mother set about lathering his skin and scalp with baby shampoo. I told her it was not necessary — babies don't need soap until they are old enough to get dirty — but Carmen smiled and nodded and nevertheless bent over her child. She wanted him *clean*. After rinsing his body thoroughly, I scooped Moises out of the water and delivered him to Carmen's waiting arms.

CARMEN AND MOISES came to stay with us after her husband beat her and turned mother and infant out of their apartment. My husband knew her family through the migrant clinic. He had already gotten to know Carmen's four brothers, who worked in the apple orchards north of Newburgh and who had paid a *coyote* to smuggled Carmen and her husband as undocumented immigrants.

Traveling jungles, mountains, and deserts, Carmen and her husband had to cross not one but two borders. Coming into Mexico, their group was robbed. But as Carmen triumphantly relates, though Mexican officials ordered them to lay all their money on the table, a crumpled bill remained hidden in her jeans pocket. If not for that oversight, they would have had no food for the rest of the trip. Arriving near the U.S. border, they were sequestered in a crowded trailer for a week while the *coyote* called Carmen's brothers to extract yet more money. On their first attempt, the group was caught and returned by *la Migra*. On their second try they crossed over. Carmen and her husband finally made it all the way to New York.

For a few months after arriving, the couple lived in a trailer along with Carmen's brothers. Their first months' wages went toward paying back the loan that had brought them across the border. But when it became clear that Carmen's husband had a drinking problem, the couple was no longer welcome. Carmen, already pregnant, could stay — provided her husband would leave. However, he convinced her that the stress of living with her brothers and the indignity of his low pay as a farmworker were driving him to drink. They decided to move off the farm and into Newburgh so that he could take a better-paying job in construction.

Moving off of the farm and away from her family, Carmen's husband promised that their relationship would improve. Carmen's eldest brother — himself a recovering alcoholic "cured" through joining a Pentecostal church — warned that it would only get worse. One Sunday at about nine o'clock after our children were tucked into bed, Carmen called from a Mexican store nearby. She had been trying to reach her brothers all day, with no luck, and the store was about to close. Could she come spend the night with us?

As the days passed, I came to love having Carmen in the house. She had a shy smile and a ready laugh that she hid behind a hand covering her mouth. Preferring to wash dishes rather than to cook (an arrangement that suited me just fine), she watched Rachel and Thomas so I could go to noon Mass. Carmen was eager to learn about parenting, a duty for which she felt unprepared for the same reason she did not know how to cook: instead of helping with domestic chores at home, she had always worked in the cornfields with her father and brothers. She described the walk from their village to the fields, watching the mist and clouds lift over the mountains, as one of the things she most missed.

Over the two weeks that Carmen and Moises stayed with us, we tried to find our way through a maze of social services. She declined going to the women's shelter my neighbors had started long ago, since without English — and without papers — she was afraid to stay there. The local battered women's agency usually has a bilingual advocate, but at that moment the previous counselor had left and they had not yet hired a new one. We investigated counseling, but not being eligible for Medicaid, Carmen could not afford the sessions.

Carmen sought *consejos* (advice from trusted individuals), rather than professional therapy, from her *padrino* (godfather) in Guatemala, her eldest brother, and others. She spoke with her mother twice — apparently just to be reassured by the sound of her voice, since she did not let on news of her predicament. (Our immigrant friends often withhold worries from family members back home until the crisis has passed.) When Carmen's husband called her to apologize, we urged her to stay with us while they worked at their relationship. Kenney told them about an Alcoholics Anonymous group and a batterers' group, both in Spanish. We asked him not to come to the house so that our home would always remain a safe space for Carmen and Moises.

I cried on the day that Carmen told us that she was leaving, that her husband had found them an apartment. I cried again after visiting them there the first time, in that dingy lineup of tenements only four blocks away on one of the most drug-infested streets of the city. "Like a lamb to the slaughter," my mind repeated. "Like a lamb to the slaughter."

We went to Moises's first birthday party — a joyous event complete with balloons, gifts, and an elaborately decorated cake paid for by Carmen's wages at a job at a coat factory. (Like others employed under false working papers, she earned under $5 an hour and she wouldn't be able to reclaim withheld taxes; she was never "given" a full week at that factory, where layoffs are commonplace.) Carmen's husband was on his best behavior at the party attended by all four of her brothers. Carmen herself shone in a new pair of jeans and a smile that showed her contentment. When she smiled she forgot to cover her mouth, and even laughed out loud as Moises shrieked when he glimpsed his birthday cake.

Around the time that Carmen became pregnant with the couple's second son, her husband went on a drinking binge. What would she do with *two* children if she had to leave him? She started to dread weekends, the only days the couple had together, but also the time when her husband drank in earnest. One afternoon, coming home from shopping, he unleashed a torrent of anger on the street. When he struck her, a watchful neighbor called the police. After going through a court-mandated anti–domestic violence program, his behavior toward her improved. And when Carmen suddenly came down with kidney troubles and had to be hospitalized, her husband turned solicitously tender toward his wife. Carmen recovered enough to be released, and later gave birth to a healthy boy. Like Moises, instead of being given the name of the saint on whose feast day he was born, he received a biblical name: Isaias.

Now having two boys, Carmen decided to stay at home rather than seek another factory job. After tax deductions, the $100 a week for daycare (at a Honduran neighbor's house) and money for carfare left her with little to show for a week of work. This gave me a chance to see more of Carmen and her boys. On hot summer days we drove to a riverside park along the shores of the Hudson River. At least there a breeze stirred the air; the sight of lapping waves and shelter of green trees cooled our skin.

Watching our children play, we commented on how much they had grown. Moises would go crazy with the excitement of playmates and the luxury of so much space to explore. Rachel couldn't understand why he tossed our picnic foods around; Thomas would complain that he threw sand. But every time I looked at Moises I remembered how, like Pharaoh's daughter, I drew him from the water.

WITHOUT LEAVING THE SAFE SHORES of one's convictions, one's language, one's self-confidence, a voyage of discovery cannot happen. Without risking new and unfamiliar territory, one cannot know what it is like to be a stranger. And without having once been a stranger, one cannot known what it means to be befriended when friendless. Kenney and I moved to Newburgh on the instinct that here, on the banks of the Hudson River in New York, we would be able to return some of the hospitality that we had received in Mexico and Central America. We moved here because we knew we would not experience the lives of the poor from the complacency of the suburbs.

In Catholic Worker philosophy, Jesus' teachings in what theologians now call the preferential option for the poor are meant to be taken seriously as essential to Christian commitment. In a consumer culture with numerous distractions to choose from, discarded people in Newburgh — people who literally aren't counted and who don't count — become invisible, segregated into pockets of poverty hidden from the public eye. Like previous generations of immigrants who served as cheap labor on farms and factories at this bend of the river, recent newcomers forge a living at the margins of an otherwise prosperous society. It becomes impossible to remember their existence — much less to enter into the reality of their suffering — if we do not place our lives nearer to theirs. We came here not knowing what shape our commitment would take, only that it had to be forged. We moved here not to become saviors, nor to lead a much-needed revolution, but because our own redemption was at stake.

Having a family of our own, I realized, we could not run a House of Hospitality (though other Catholic Worker parents — including my own — have shown that it can be done). But we *could* open our home — and our hearts. By cultivating relationships, we are all changed. Rachel and Thomas have taught Moises to play more gently. I have learned to watch Carmen make her own decisions.

ONE DAY THREE YEARS AFTER that first night Carmen had spent at our home, she showed up on our doorstep, distraught and exhausted. Her husband had not worked for two weeks, and he had been drinking. Finally she had had enough. She decided to embark on a step toward freedom. Once he fell asleep, she packed up a bag of clothes and diapers and took off walking with the boys. He had not hit her, she reassured us; but she decided to leave when she sensed that soon he would.

Carmen sat all that afternoon in the rocking chair, too spent to soothe the baby's cries or to control her toddler's boisterous activity. That night, her youngest brother picked them up and took them out to the trailer on the farm. When Carmen went back after months away, it was because her husband had changed. Her brothers had been going to the apartment for four-hour, deadly serious conversations with him. After work, he began spending more time with churchgoing recovering alcoholics instead of with heavy-drinking bachelors. The couple went to the minister of the Pentecostal church for *consejos*. Carmen's husband's own younger brother and sister — Pentecostals who do not drink alcohol — had come across the border. Their company seemed to lighten the mood of the apartment, and their earnings, chipped in toward the bills, lessened the couple's economic woes.

The family recently moved to a more spacious apartment just up the block. This year Moises entered preschool — an outlet for the energy that he possesses in abundance — and his behavior has improved. Carmen hardly seems the same person as the shy, frightened young woman just finding her way in Newburgh; her smile no longer covered by a timid hand, she no longer hides her laugh.

Stigmata

> *My hands and feet have shriveled;*
> *I can count all my bones.*
> — *Psalm 22*

I had pieced together the strands of Newburgh's past to understand its identity; but I had not realized that, even more importantly, I needed to pay attention to its present — especially the present hidden from public view. Only by studying the river's daily variations could I claim to capture its changing beauty; only by exploring the lives of people like Carmen could I glimpse the city's hidden treasure. A larger perspective had put the small betrayals I had suffered as a teenager returning here into their proper context — the story of a city with a long history of betrayal. But they could be healed only by witnessing other people's sufferings in the present: listening to the stories of contemporary settlers on the river's banks.

Occupying the same seat at the bakery window from which I had first spotted Karen's mother, I glanced past the swinging doors into the kitchen with its stacks of metal trays and huge ovens and realized that this Italian bakery is now staffed by Mexicans. The father of another of our catechism students works here, where he says the owner treats him well and, after so many years, he earns decent money. At another bakery across the river, however, an undocumented worker lost a finger while operating one of the bread-slicing machines.

The bakery owner, known by word-of-mouth to hire recently arrived immigrants without papers, promised the injured worker he would pay all related medical bills. Although the finger was lost for good, the worker, a young man with a wife and small child, felt fortunate to receive medical treatment and to have a job to return to. But when hospital invoices began to arrive and he brought them to his boss, the bakery owner declared that not only would he not pay the bills — the young man was fired. If he dared to complain, the boss threatened, he could do so to the I.N.S., since he would call to have him deported. Not only did the worker have to figure out what to do about the medical bills and look for another job; he had to decide whether to move his family from their apartment, since the owner knew where they lived.

Although my husband referred the young man to a lawyer and encouraged him to file a worker's compensation case, nothing came of it. Without pay stubs or proof of any kind that he had worked at that particular bakery (the workers there are paid only in cash), opening a case would have been difficult to do. Only the testimony of co-workers could establish the facts, and the young man was unwilling to put them in danger since they too are undocumented. By testifying against the boss, they would undoubtedly lose their jobs; there was also the chance, he feared, that they too might be deported.

While his injury is more extreme than some others — and more infuriating because it holds no promise of compensation — there are many such stories to be heard in the valley. The river's banks are full of stories of suffering and struggle, like Carmen's. They resound with injustice committed against those too vulnerable to seek recourse, but they echo too a subtle determination.

By listening closely to the testimonies of recent immigrants to my hometown, I have detected, as well, an unexpected silver chord — the reverberation of an inherent solidarity. Nonsensical as they may seem, strategies for survival sometimes defy reason. A wronged young man refuses to put his companions at risk, even if it means abandoning his chance for compensation. The well-being of her children forms the motive for Carmen's staying or leaving an abusive relationship. Their testimonies allure, hidden treasure to be heard for the listening. Like a warrior's death chant, they signal the persistent refusal to accept defeat; like stigmata, they show evidence of an ongoing Passion.

** *Six* **

Settling In

A single golden thread courses through me, fine as a fishing line treasured in a little girl's pocket as her older brother rescues her from a rank, gushing creek emptying into the river. Vibrant and alive as a pulse, it drifts and sometimes disappears into the narrative of my life; at other times it sits plainly on the surface. Its silky tension relaxes into an expansive arc or pulls taut, sharp and cutting as a knife's edge. In order to be cast, the line must be let go, allowing its invisible end to extend beyond one's grasp.

Beyond prediction or control, the day's catch may yield an old boot or a rusted rearview mirror as easily as an impressive fish. What really matters is never to lose the feel of the single golden thread clasped in the fingers, in hands that must open and close freely without letting the line get away completely. Losing grasp of it would be a worse tragedy than being pulled headfirst into scummy water. Losing it means losing my life. My real life. My inner life. A life awakened on the Bluff and along a chilly creek gushing into the Hudson River.

Every afternoon as I drive my daughter to or from school, we pass the street frequented by prostitutes a few blocks from our house. They pace up and down in front of the shelter begun in the building donated by Nicole and Ruby's parents, which we fixed up so long ago. I wish I could claim that each time I pass the women I feel a pang of compassion, but the truth is that I have gotten used to seeing them and barely take notice. Recognizing a prostitute's face on the front page of the local newspaper, at the same moment I realized that I haven't seen her lately. She wandered streets and sidewalks indiscriminately. (I worried she would walk into a moving car.) She walked with attitude, holding her body saucily and sporting skimpy outfits, while her face betrayed the not-quite-there gaze of an addict. On Easter Monday she was murdered: she was struck over the head with a blunt instrument, and her body was set on fire in the park across the street from my daughter's school.

Newspaper reports revealed that the woman, Cathy, came from a large, troubled family. I learned that she was two years older than me and that she had been in my brother's high school class. The circumstances that led her into drug addiction and prostitution were not addressed in much detail, but I wondered if abuse had played a role. A surprisingly enlightened editorial by the current city manager decried the lack of funding for drug rehabilitation programs and pointed to prostitution's wider context. Cathy's integrity had already been desecrated. Seeing her skin exposed in tacky clothing, we had not glimpsed her true identity. But this final desecration shocked us — rightly — into seeing her humanity. She too was somebody's daughter. She too is a child of God.

As a parent, I often struggle with the demands for my full attention as I raise our children. This struggle has not diminished over time but, on the contrary, has intensified, as my "new mother" excitement fades as my energy wanes with age. The days of relishing hours of staring into Rachel's face or standing rapt in awe of each faltering baby step seems distant to present reality.

Whereas each signal of Rachel's development, no matter how tiny, evoked fascination, and each landmark of Thomas's growth prompted comparison, Seamus's evolution unfolds quietly. Once Rachel has been delivered to kindergarten and Thomas to nursery school, I rock Seamus to sleep with lullabies. Some days I would rather get an article in the mail or tackle some chore in the house, but when this pleasant duty wins out, I am glad. Together we are shoring up closeness tucked into his golden cells like treasure. He will not remember these moments consciously, but without them he would be hampered in future intimacy. Inevitably, he will need to call upon this investment of comfort, even as he grows away from me. And, for a change, I can give him my full attention.

Once when reprimanded for falling asleep during prayer, Thérèse of Lisieux replied, "A child is equally pleasing to her parent whether asleep or awake." To rest in the knowledge that one is never alone, that a loving Mother/Father God holds us in constant view, is a security each child has a right to know. Prayer is about paying attention. Suddenly one wakes up to become aware of a God who, like a good Mother, is already present. Thus, prayer does not so much put us in the presence of God as forge a reciprocal bond of attention.

Simone Weil wrote that what was missing from the political movements of her time was the quality of paying attention. Dorothy Day cautioned that while advocacy and organizing are necessary to a Christian community's commitment, they must arise from direct personal encounters with the poor in which people are seen as fully human. We are afraid to sit with the discomfort of unmasked misery. We rush past the works of mercy as I rushed past Cathy in my car. But it is precisely in these encounters that conversion takes place.

I do not regret passing Cathy on my way to drop off Rachel at school; after all, it would have been inappropriate to accost her on the street, asking her to unveil her vulnerability to a stranger. Furthermore, her story is just one among those of many, many broken people we come across in daily life here in this run-down city. I do ask myself, however, if I can do a better job of paying attention in my relationships. How can I better engage in acts of loving comfort so that others can feel lulled by God's parental mercy? And I question all of us, why did we wait until Cathy's death to see her humanity? As a woman is laid to rest during Easter Week, entering the loving arms of a God whose daughter has come home, I pray for her peace and for our unquiet.

Hospitality

When the owner of our building decided he would move permanently to the farm he had just bought farther north, he gave up his couch in the back of the used book store. Clearing out two dumpster containers' worth of moldy books, vacant canning jars, and miscellaneous pieces of rotten wood (held on to "just in case"), he left us the house, with the offer to hold an interest-free mortgage for us at a price that fancy people might pay for a new car. We debated whether or not to buy it; my husband knew enough about home repair to recognize the house was as much a liability as an asset. But we suspected that we would probably lose access to the garden space if a new owner — especially an absentee slumlord — took over. We wondered whether the downstairs or upstairs floors would be rented to trustworthy tenants. We knew our rent would go up.

The apartment above ours was rented to an elderly white woman who reminded me of Karen's mother. A widow and retired schoolteacher, she had lived in Newburgh for decades and counted herself among that dying breed who refused to leave. She too wandered the streets during the day, although I don't think she would be caught collecting cans. And, like Karen's mother, her memory and reason seemed to be fading. She often took an inexplicable dislike to unknown men, such as the new letter carrier — and unfortunately, my husband.

When we asked the previous owner about it, he just scratched his head and confessed that he did not know what *he* had done to deserve her recriminations either. While I was able to get away with "Good morning" or "Excuse me" without reprisals in the hallway, my husband was not so lucky. He had offended her sensibilities in some way we could never figure out. To his greeting one afternoon as they passed each other, she harrumphed and spat out, "Sap!" Bewildered (and tempted to laugh out loud), he kept quiet. By the next time her level of disdain had escalated to sarcasm: "Oh, good day to you too, *Mister* Sap!" But the most puzzling was an unexpectedly threatening response to his third attempt to be neighborly: "How are you going to like it in jail, Mr. Sap?" We tried to coax her into friendliness with cookies, dutifully delivered by the children, or by helping carry groceries up the stairs, but she deemed these gestures intrusive.

The elderly woman upstairs did not last long in the building after we bought it. One day she fell while out walking and broke her hip. Secluding herself for several days, she avoided seeking medical treatment. After police officers came one evening to check on her, since she had not been answering the phone and her daughter had finally called the police, the poor woman was finally convinced to enter a retirement home. Her daughter and her family came from farther north on the other side of the river and arranged the move. We were glad for our elderly neighbor that family members had finally claimed her, since in three years we had not seen her receive any visitors, but we were sad to think that it took a crisis for them to attend to her needs.

HAVING THE UPSTAIRS APARTMENT VACANT, we experimented with offering short-term respite for other people going through transitions. For the price of the apartment's maintenance costs (about half of the going market rate), we rented it to people we knew needed a place to live. A peace activist from Honduras, whom I knew through the Grail women's movement to which we both belong, had unexpectedly been forced to seek refuge in the United States. I had admired Rosalba for her commitment to social justice since meeting her at a conference in Mexico ten years ago. (She works with prisoners and torture victims.) She had kept in regular contact with our women's movement, taking part in several international exchanges, until unforeseen circumstances forced her to seek asylum in this country. Rosalba lived with us while making other living and work arrangements.

Taking English classes and pursuing her immigration case took up much of Rosalba's time. Her most demanding task, however, came with our third child's birth. Rosalba took charge of caring for baby Seamus and me during my *cuarenta días* (forty days), the customary time to assist women who have given birth. Offering hospitality, we found that it was she who became the caretaker. The respite we tried to provide for her turned into forty days during which she accompanied *us* in *our* need. For that moment, our two separate desert journeys came together in one sojourn.

When Rosalba became Seamus's godmother, his baptism gave her "another reason to go on living." It seemed to make sense that she become his *madrina* (godmother). The sacraments, after all, imitate domestic life as they create a liturgical space that is both intimate and communal. The works of mercy (feeding, clothing, encouraging, instructing, burying, washing, reprimanding, etc.) take their cue from the kinship experiences of flesh-and-blood people who undertake them every day, day after day — becoming family in an enlarged sense of the word. I was reminded of Dorothy and Peter, for the Catholic Worker vision that insists that no one remain outside of the circle, and thankful to the Grail movement that brought us together.

Our upstairs apartment was occupied next by a young couple who had just gotten married. Eduardo, a nephew of one of the farmworkers my husband knows best, was a bright, capable student. He studied in medical school for three years before coming to the United States. Perhaps we were predisposed to like him since he came from just outside the elegant colonial city where we lived. His family, originally from a different state (one of the poorest in Mexico), had moved to a recently settled *colonia* on its outskirts. Although they did find more opportunities in the city than in the rural area, they also realized they could not keep up with the expenses required for his studies.

Arriving here with his younger brother, Eduardo learned English quickly. Soon he made himself indispensable at the farm store where he assumed extra responsibilities. But when he fell in love with and married a young woman, the grower would not allow the wife to live on the farm if she did not work there; and she did not intend to quit her job at a migrant daycare center. There were no suitable accommodations for another couple, anyway. They lived with us while the young woman's parents renovated a small house on their property. Eduardo became my husband's *ahijado* (godson) when he asked Kenney to be his sponsor for the sacrament of confirmation. Once again, by offering the works of mercy, we were the ones who found ourselves blessed.

Eduardo and his young wife taught us another lesson: while we prided ourselves on extending the works of mercy, we were actually joining an entire community that was already putting them into practice — in a less obtrusive way. When his cousin separated from her alcoholic boyfriend, Eduardo invited her to stay with them in the apartment upstairs. She stayed with them for several weeks until she figured out what to do next. Kenney and I laughed that Eduardo and his wife had beat us at "doing hospitality." Immigrants themselves, they offered their home to the more recently arrived.

Gardens

During the growing season, my husband and I hosted garden projects for the kids we taught in catechism. Without even knowing the name of this ecological school of thought, the previous owner had implemented a Permaculture system. Fruit trees, compost piles, a henhouse, wooded "wild" space, and two organic garden plots translated into a miniature homestead capable of growing some thirty kinds of fruits and vegetables in small quantities. The chickens were the biggest hit for the kids who helped in the garden. Our own children learned to collect freshly laid eggs from the coop.

Oftentimes our Latino friends and neighbors from rural backgrounds were delighted to find *gringos* who too valued fresh produce (we grew *epazote, cilantro,* and *jalapeños* to share) and who were trying to teach children what life might look like outside of an urban environment. They had grown up on a farm but their own children, raised here in the city, had never heard a rooster crow or seen a *milpa* (cornfield) grow. One girl's father worked as an organizer for a *campesino* organization in Mexico. As we walked through the garden, he identified each sprouting plant or fruit tree by name. The only one he could not name was rhubarb (not a common plant in Mexico).

Extra hands and practical advice (e.g., which vegetables make good neighbors and which ones don't — *"no conviven"*) were indispensable to us, since neither my husband nor I have a green thumb or much gardening experience. Working with kids, I learned that if I wanted to be a positive influence for them, I had to include (not replace) their parents. As a white person from the dominant culture, I realized that if we did not make it clear that their families and the backgrounds they come from are to be respected, we would be unconsciously repeating the same racist cycle that distances kids from their own communities. Ultimately, such a model cannot foster the self-esteem that will buffer them from drugs, gangs, and inappropriate relationships. Welcoming their parents became a way of validating the wisdom their families had brought with them but that is not ordinarily valued in this highly developed country — especially not in this urban setting.

House Work

I think of Peter Maurin every time I sweep. Since two adults, three small children, a dog, and a steady stream of visitors kick up a lot of dust, I recall this French peasant and co-founder of the Catholic Worker often. Taking a broom to the floors of our little apartment lulls me into a reflection on Peter's insistence on manual labor, his distrust of technology.

True to one of those unwritten laws of family life, a principle of chaos theory, the mess is neither created nor destroyed, it simply moves around faster than I can get to it. If the house is clean, the garden must be a mess of unruly weeds and unharvested vegetables. If both of these are in good shape, then it must be the car that is full of odd socks, used-up juice boxes, and the cadavers of peanut butter and jelly sandwiches.

Lately the same principle applies to our household appliances. First the stove went. I had been trying to convince my husband, Kenney, that I smelled a gas leak. Since his training is in plumbing and mine in theology, his opinion usually carries more weight in practical matters. But in a rare case of reversal, I relished one of those "I told you so" moments that must be survived by every good marriage. A technician using an electronic beeper that began to sound off frantically as he approached the kitchen found no fewer than five gas leaks. It's a good thing this old house is so drafty, he informed us. Skeptically eyeing the grease-encrusted stove that came with this once-abandoned house, he recommended buying a new model. It would be cheaper than trying to fix the old one.

Next went the refrigerator. Its power would shut off inexplicably and then just as mysteriously click on again. Kenney checked out books from the library and read that when the compressor begins to fail, it's time to start saving for a new refrigerator. In the meantime, we employed another one of those unwritten principles: sometimes an appliance, like a person, just needs a rest. (In fact, this discovery may be responsible for our engagement: stuck in a car that would not shift gears, trapped in a downpour on a shantytown's dirt road in Mexico, I amazed my future husband on our first date by suggesting we turn off the engine. Stunned by my automotive wisdom, he asked me for a second date.) This strategy worked for several months. Even our three-year-old son learned to recognize the sound that meant the compressor needed a break. But one day as we poured milk into our coffee and yogurt came out instead, we knew our appliance karma would no longer be cheated. Replacing the refrigerator turned out to be more complicated than buying a new stove. A search for a good used fridge led to unmarked storefronts and a junk guru's backyard.

The dryer was the last appliance to go. This dryer had been donated to us by the Sisters next door, and it had sat unused in the basement while we debated what to do with it. Used to clotheslines, we also hesitated to use products made by General Electric. The ideal of how we want to live and the reality of our situation contradict each other. But with the onset of winter and our third child's birth, we dreaded washing and hanging out cloth diapers in addition to the rest of the week's laundry. In the end, we kept it. My husband again checked a handyman's book out of the library and hooked it up himself. We made it through winter before the dryer gave way, its faltering motor being the reason it had been donated in the first place. Now we have to figure out what to do with a defunct dryer.

When they bought a new vacuum cleaner, the Sisters offered us their old one. Though baby Seamus, who was then crawling, looked like a dust mop, it was easy to decline. I think of the family I stayed with in Nicaragua and of our friends in *colonias* in Mexico, remembering how they wet down the floors with a broom each morning. I imagine the woman in St. Luke's Gospel sweeping her house in search of the lost coin. A broom will never break down. It's inexpensive to replace. It does not require fossil fuel, nor will it pollute when its useful life is over. A masterpiece of appropriate technology, it was not made in sweatshops, nor are wars being fought over its source of energy.

Dorothy Day, the other co-founder of the Catholic Worker, remarked that once you no longer experience poverty as a daily reality, it is easy to forget what it looks like. Living simply allows us a glimpse of holy poverty: daily reminders of the world's poor; utter dependence on creation; trust in God instead of in our own ability to control; the ultimate in ecological sustainability. It opens the door to a God who understands our inadequacies and who greets us in all our contradictions, even coming out to meet us, broom in hand.

The Pueblo *Upstairs*

Our most recent tenants — a married couple, their two children, and the wife's brother — put in our garden last year. As *campesinos* from Mexico, they know more about the land than we do. Reymundo has worked here for five years; before New York, he worked in Tennessee, and before that, in California. (His older brother was one of the inhabitants of a squatter camp that attracted national attention to the situation of border areas: working in the construction boom in the San Diego area, but not earning enough to afford housing themselves, they took over a hillside and built dwellings out of leftover scraps of wood. By the time they were discovered by authorities, hundreds of Mexican and Central American workers lived there.)

Reymundo found his way to New York through his wife's brother, who works on an apple farm just north of Newburgh. My husband got to know this family when Reymundo's brother-in-law fell out of a tree and had to go to the clinic where Kenney worked. Soon after, Reymundo convinced his wife, Laura, to join him in New York, and she and her youngest brother, Manuel, crossed the border with Alicia, age six, and José, then just two.

Reymundo, having been here already, was somewhat used to this country; Laura, however, had to adjust. At first she cried every day, missing the tiny, isolated village where she grew up. But she preferred being here with Reymundo to staying behind with her two young children while he worked in the United States. Their village is home to many women whose husbands never came home, having stayed away so long they never wanted to return to the *pueblo* or having found new wives in *el Norte*.

In the *pueblo*, our neighbors grew up without a gas stove or refrigerator; when I asked Laura (an excellent cook) how to prepare a dish, she used to begin each recipe, "First you have to go out and cut the wood. . . . " Even though Laura reads and writes (she and Reymundo both completed sixth grade — the legal requirement in Mexico) and even though the paperwork is sent to her in Spanish, she struggles through the copious forms necessary for keeping up with the children's schools or procuring their health care. Our children and theirs, constant companions, teach each other English and Spanish in a felicitous exchange.

Manuel, unlike his sister and brother-in-law, neither reads nor writes. Born premature (his mother used to tell the story of how he fit in a shoebox), he spent a sheltered childhood and went out only to accompany his father in the fields. Manuel came here for the same reasons other people go to college: to make a name for himself, to get ahead economically, to do something with his life. Too shy to approach girls, Manuel is not yet married. With so few eligible young women here (like in Newburgh at the turn of the century), he plans to return to the *pueblo* to find a wife. In a migrant version of arranged marriages, his parents will seek a girl willing to accept the trade-off of a husband who leaves seasonally but whose economic means surpasses that of other suitors.

Manuel and Reymundo work up to sixty hours a week in a fabric-dyeing factory. They leave for work at three o'clock in the morning and return in the afternoon after a twelve-hour shift. Since they are such good workers, they earned the privilege of extra hours on Sunday, when they clean the machines. Their job is tedious, since it mostly entails operating machines that do the dyeing, but it can be dangerous. Once Reymundo let his attention drift and the huge rollers that rotate as they dye the cloth caught hold of his sweatshirt. The material of his clothing being so thick it could not be ripped, he found himself being sucked into the two huge rollers of the machine. As he braced himself with his hands, his ribs were bruised as he resisted being crushed in the machinery. Fortunately Manuel was there to flip the switch and turn off the power.

The long-term damage to Reymundo and Manuel's health may be caused not by accidents but by the toxins of the chemicals used in the dyeing process. Clouds of colors drift through the air of the plant; although there are ventilators, the air never really gets cleared. While the workers are offered face masks, most do not use them, finding them a nuisance. Besides, they don't plan to be here very long. Reymundo and Manuel have been employed at the factory for over two years, but they see their stint there as temporary.

My husband and I laugh when we ascend the stairs to the upstairs apartment, joking that we are going to the village in Michoacán. Unlike Eduardo, who looks forward to a future here and occasionally glances back at the past in Mexico — and unlike Rosalba, who looks back often to Honduras but knows she *must* stay here — the family is caught between two worlds. Not really immigrants, since they do not intend to stay, they are not migrants, either, since Reymundo no longer moves around. When they use the word *acá* (here), they mean their home country; they still speak of the *pueblo* in the present tense. Social events in

141

the village take precedence over occurrences here. Wiring a day's worth of wages, they pay for rapid mail service to deliver video-tapes of the latest parties in the *pueblo*. (Filming for loved ones in *el Norte* has become a cottage industry.) The festivities represent not single events, but a whole community coming home.

Many of those villagers — mostly the young — who strayed to Mexico City, Tennessee, or California have come to the village for the occasion. The party will last until sunrise the next day; food, beer, and soda will be offered to everyone who arrives; music will blare from loudspeakers incessantly. Listening for their names to be announced on the microphone by the emcee of this huge, outdoor party attended by the whole village, Laura, Manuel, and Reymundo hear *saludos* (greetings) being sent to them by video. *Padrinos* (sponsors) of the party, who contributed U.S. dollars for the festivities, they have become something of celebrities.

Once their own house is finished, Reymundo and Laura claim, they will be returning. But months turn into years, and leaving will not be easy. Here, health care and education are within easier reach than in their impoverished area of Mexico. Jobs here may be backbreaking, tedious, and even dangerous, but they get paid more in one hour than their cousins (who work for the U.S.-based agribusiness that bought up the village's communally owned land) earn in a day. Coming home, they watch the videos over meals prepared with foods bought in the Mexican grocery store or brought back by the acquaintance who made the latest trip home. Arguing about who's who, they tell and retell stories about the characters on the screen.

There's the *muchacho* who was born with *virtud* (in this use, an ability to foretell the future) but who, they explain, had it taken away by the village *brujo* (sorcerer). There's their cousin, just back from cutting tobacco in Tennessee, or another, returned in disgrace after selling drugs in Southern California. There's the mother of the neighbor who disappeared while crossing the border, swept away in the river and never seen again. Eyes set on their homeland, bodies physically present in New York, Laura, Reymundo, and Manuel have forged an uneasy truce with Newburgh.

Caught between exodus and exile, they may reside here, but their real lives are lived somewhere else.

Real Presence

> *My heart is steadfast, O God,*
> *my heart is steadfast.*
> — *Psalm 57*

Like our neighbors upstairs, in my own way I had not been fully present here. Internally I had resisted settling in, considering my return to a city I had long ago given up on as an inconsequential coincidence. It took me a while to see that coming back to New-burgh gave me the opportunity to make my peace with this city, not simply a truce. However, as hard as I tried by my own efforts to achieve this peace, I could not. It had to be given to me.

LATE AT NIGHT, probably around two o'clock in the morning, we were awakened by an argument taking place just outside our window. The midweek party crowd from the seedy dance club around the corner had just spilled out. A man and a woman con-tested back and forth. The man's voice, too low to hear distinctly, was threatening and insistent, while the woman's voice, panic-stricken, could be heard clearly repeating over and over, "I don't have it. I don't have it." They argued back and forth, he demand-ing the goods or the money she was obviously supposed to be carrying and she repeating her sole piteous phrase. If he didn't believe her, she begged, he could check her pockets.

As we roused ourselves, having already lost sleep because of the loud music blasting from around the corner, we could hear the desperation mounting. Stumbling toward the window, my hus-band pulled back the curtain to look down from our second story apartment. From there, he saw the man knock the woman down, straddle her, and hold a knife to her throat. By the time I made it to the phone to call the police and my husband rushed to the door to go downstairs, two passersby had already intervened. Looking as if they were returning from a night shift at a factory, they were dressed in work clothes and carried thermoses.

These two unlikely Good Samaritans took the assailant by surprise. Whisking the knife from his hand, they pulled him off of the woman. She scrambled to her feet to run and they restrained him in order to give her a good head start. He cursed at them, but it was plain that they did not understand what he was saying. When police sirens sounded, responding to my call, the two young men took off running as well. Young Latino men who do not speak English and who do not have legal status might not be automatically considered Good Samaritans, but criminals. The woman too ran *from* the police instead of running *toward* them for help, and so I knew that her problems went back farther than that particular assault. All night and the following day, her pitiful voice, high-pitched in desperation, resounded in my ears.

WHEN WE MOVED to Newburgh, my husband and I knew we would be confronting a shadow side of society that most of us don't want to remember exists. But if we lived here in name only and did not actively witness the daily life of our neighbors, we would also fail in being present. Living here has given us the opportunity to witness the violence of drug culture and interpersonal abuse. It has also given us the gift of a glimpse of two Good Samaritans, themselves foreigners here, risking themselves to rescue a stranger.

Another late-night argument comes to mind, one that took place between a couple who were briefly our neighbors. Dragged once again from sleep by the sound of voices rising in pitch and intensity, this time we heard the man's voice but not the woman's. He ranted and raved while berating a woman, and if she made a reply I could not catch it. Not trying to eavesdrop, but rather kept from sleep by their altercation, I had already begun to judge them in my mind; I assumed they were a prostitute and pimp. Eventually it became clear that they were a husband and wife who had gone out to their front stoop to argue so they would not wake their sleeping children inside.

This time it was the man's voice, thickened with desperation, that resounded in my mind afterward. He argued his case to her: he worked himself to the bone only to come home and find that his kids hadn't been given supper; she had no money for groceries, having spent it all on crack. He repeated his refrain helplessly: "I *told* you to quit them drugs." The family moved out soon after. A heap of belongings on the sidewalk announced their flight.

MONDAY MORNINGS one often finds in the city streets hapless piles of belongings, as if an apartment had been suddenly, mysteriously emptied: mattresses, children's toys, toiletries, papers, junked televisions or stereos, piles of clothes jumbled in a heap. Old armchairs or kitchen tables, battered dressers or even appliances might be dumped on the curb. A backpack, seemingly brand new, might be among the mess, and one can't help but wonder. Did it belong to a boy or a girl? Were any important school notices or homework left inside? Would its owner be going back to school, and did he or she have another one?

One drives or walks past such piles of belongings on the curb and wonders what happened. The sheer incongruity of it — and the regularity of these occurrences — jars me. It looks as if a sudden evacuation had been necessary, as if someone had to flee with no time to pack. The many articles that compose a living household's daily reality lay on the curb, one more pile of junk, abandoned.

Gift

Some days I drive or walk past the river and my heart suddenly contracts with a pang of contrition for not having noticed its changes in color. Their immensity ignites the smallness of my soul with a wordless desire; their variable colors, which never look quite the same on two consecutive days, awaken an unnameable, enormous capacity to trust that a seamlessly shifting universe will fulfill its promise of fulfillment, peace, beauty. The river and mountains and sky have not lapsed in their ability to communicate to me this everlasting reality. It is, rather, my attention that has failed.

Attention: the simplest, cheapest, most accessible of gifts, yet so difficult to bestow. Attention heals. Attention transforms. Children cannot thrive without it. Plants and animals mysteriously respond to it. Specialists tell us that victims of trauma or those under psychological stress can become incapable of harnessing it. Drug or alcohol abusers lose it, eroded, and adults who never received it as children find it extremely hard to grant. Material items, food, television, and other distractions are easy substitutes for what cannot be replaced: deep, authentic attention.

My children have taught me the most about the importance of attention. True attention, of course, cannot be achieved in "quality time" spent in fifteen-minute increments meant to make up for absenting one's self for the rest of the day, ignoring or neglecting this vastly huge hunger with which children are born. Like Peter Maurin's formulation of personalism, rooted in philosophy but instilled in the Catholic Worker as an eminently practical teaching, quality attention rests on the dignity of the human person.

Attention can come in an "aha" moment, and those moments come even to the least disciplined, the most irresponsible, the severely distracted — or even deluded — among us. In cultivating awareness we can be more free and open to receive those grace-filled moments. We cannot control when or where or how or why we "get" them, and we cannot control the fact that they may be "squandered" on those whom we judge the least likely. (In the Gospels, Jesus often shocks his hearers by saying that prostitutes and tax collectors would enter the Reign of God before Pharisees.) But we *do* know that these moments *will* come if we are living close to God's truth for us — and that, like children, they are worth rearranging our lives for.

Just because one lives a life of integrity — even a radical one — one cannot expect grace as one's due. But living a radical life of integrity, what God demands so lovingly from each of us, *can* create an openness in our hearts to respond to contemplative moments.

When we follow the vocation God plants deeply, mysteriously inside each of us, an internal stress, an invisible, interior resistance, is abated. The energy we spent pushing away God's will (daily, yearly — in patterns set over a lifetime) can be freed up to hone the attention. One's gaze can then rest more authentically — and more compassionately — on others and the natural world.

It HAD RAINED all morning, but now the sun had just come out. From the sink I watched the children playing outside on the other side of the window pane. Rachel chattered away in Spanish with Alicia as they dressed dolls dragged out on the patio. Thomas, squeezed into the plastic car donated by the doctor at Kenney's clinic, steered around in circles. Little José was busily digging up some stuffed animals buried in the yard. We never seem to get the vegetable beds planted as early as I would like, but the garden was already growing faster than could be kept up with. My husband, at work, would arrive home late with stories to tell — stories for which I would wait up, to feed my greedy curiosity and to hear how the folks on the farms were doing.

Suddenly, something happened that made me catch my breath. In the wire mesh around the patio, a single crystal drop of rain lingered in each lower right-hand corner of each tiny square of fence. The late afternoon sun unscrolled its shimmering body across the back porch, setting each raindrop ablaze with pure, immaculate light. I stood transfixed as rows and rows of diamonds embedded in the one swatch of fencing on which the sun fell glittered on my back porch. I stood in awe before a wealth of jewels, a store of treasure.

That was the week a dead man's body was discovered in a vacant lot around the corner. The neighborhood drug dealers were working overtime now that warm weather had come. Our Iraq vigil group had started up again after a long winter, and my husband would soon bring home new narratives in the ongoing sagas of farmworkers whose lives he could only slightly, momentarily improve. Spring rain leaking into the ceiling informed us that we needed to patch the roof — again. I had spent much of the afternoon daydreaming about remodeling I knew we'd never be able to afford.

And yet, this unexpected glimpse of beauty, this perfection of sun and water in a ruined city, reminded me that God was fully, magnificently present. Before the dishwater drained, I had to acknowledge this gift. Stopped by unutterable joy, I clutched the side of the sink and tried to whisper the gratitude that rose to my throat. I had never been so perfectly happy before in my life.

> *How lovely is your dwelling place,*
> *O Lord of hosts!*
> *My soul longs, indeed it faints*
> *for the courts of the Lord;*
> *my heart and my flesh sing for joy*
> *to the living God.*
>
> *Even the sparrow finds a home,*
> *and the swallow a nest for herself,*
> *where she may lay her young,*
> *at your altars, my Ruler and my God.*
> *Happy are those who live in your house,*
> *ever singing your praise.*
>
> *— Psalm 84*

** *Seven* **

Manna

It's Pentecost, and also the day of my third child's baptism. My husband and I escape the humid heat, glad to take refuge in the sheltering cool of our parish church. Friends, family, and co-workers are there to accompany us on this, the day our son enters life in Christ. Here come my parents and brother from the Catholic Worker farm. In wanders Mike, the man who collects our cans. Cousins from the suburbs sit sedately in pews. Farmworkers arrive dressed in their Sunday best. Friends from the nine Latin American countries of origin of our parish pause to light a candle or touch a statue. It's Pentecost, the church's birthday. As to any good party, here comes everybody.

This baptism is truly a family affair. Held by his godmother, who is here from Honduras to be treated for AIDS and now lives in our household, Seamus wears a christening gown passed down in my husband's family for generations. My father, a deacon, delights in his role as presider. Rachel and Thomas stand on tiptoe to trace the sign of the cross on their baby brother's forehead. My husband — partner in late-night vigils, referee of sibling rivalry, my sanity during toddler temper tantrums — stands at my side. Both the sweltering heat and the composition of the crowd remind me of our wedding day, and I rejoice in the font of grace from which these young lives have burst forth.

Oblivious to its ancient symbolism and poetic grandeur, Seamus receives the sacrament, unabashedly pleased to be the center of attention. His chest, smooth and luminous as wax, is anointed with chrism; his beautifully round skull is bathed with water; his last patch of cradle cap is caressed with oil; his rosebud

149

mouth, bright blue eyes, and newly unfolding ears are opened and blessed. Lit from the Paschal flame, his slender baptismal candle is entrusted to his godfather. And so, cleansed with water and sealed with oil, Seamus is named priest, prophet, and king. He is *christened.*

As this great wider family welcomes my son, I am surprised by a swift, sudden pang of loss. Even as Seamus gurgles, sings, and finally squeals with laughter, I am mourning. My body had cradled him for nine months, and since birth we have been inseparable. I took him to my job at the Grail Center, lugging his car seat to meetings, talks, and programs. We hibernated together through January snowfalls and snuggled on the back porch during spring rains. We slept in the same bed and nestled for naps in our big rocking chair. When I stroked his back or jiggled him on my knee to bring up air bubbles, invariably I would burp as well. Whatever I ate or drank, he tasted in my milk. My body alone has sustained him with food, warmth, comfort.

But soon he will be eating foods other than my milk; he no longer rejects my half-hearted attempts to feed him cereal. Already he responds to his sister and brother as much as to me; he can't wait to wriggle out of my arms and onto the floor with them. His infant days are over. And having been through this twice before, I know that this is only the first in a long series of departures. This baptism signals the separateness of his one, holy life.

The Gospel of Luke tells of a small-town boy come home to announce his one, holy life (4:14–21). In a perfectly framed narrative, Jesus reads from Isaiah's Jubilee passage proclaiming a year of favor from the Lord. And he adds, "This reading has been fulfilled in your midst." I can imagine the hush of cousins, friends, and neighbors, and then, their indignant reaction. Such a revelation from one who has grown up among them! In a village inhabited by only a handful of families, he stands there, strangely alone in the midst of those who have known and loved him.

Seamus too will startle all of us who love him. Although he looks just like Rachel and Thomas, who look just like my husband's family and mine, his life is an unfolding revelation, unseen, unknown. We have welcomed him into our family but now we welcome him into a wider family, one based not on familiarity but rather on the newness of Pentecost. On the same Spirit who descended in the desert to seal the covenant with an entire people — men, women, and children — and who poured out newness on those gathered in Jerusalem for the Feast of Weeks.

During the baptism party at our house, English and Spanish speakers struggled to understand each other. The musicians arrive late, which is just as well given their distinctly atonal performance. Since it is an oppressively hot day, the guests are insatiably thirsty and we run out of drinks. A sudden thunderstorm strikes and rain dribbles into the kitchen through the leaky roof we have not yet managed to fix. Nevertheless, surrounded by everybody accompanying us through the chaotic blessings of family life, I find the presence of mind to rejoice in Seamus's baptism. Grieving at my loss, I celebrate his birth into the Mystical Body. Mourning his separateness, I delight in the beauty of this icon of Christ. I deliver him to his vocation, and he brings me to mine: reborn in water, fire, Spirit, we arrive together to a threshold we must each cross over, alone.

Agape

Eight miles north of Newburgh, the view changes completely. The proportions of land to sky and water have already shifted into a new configuration. Green-shouldered mountains stand dressed in a rolling skirt that unfolds into waves at their feet. From here, Bannerman's Island is visible only as a distant landmark, whereas in Newburgh the mysterious island dominates the landscape in the imagination. The Newburgh-Beacon bridge stretches out at an unfamiliar angle, at my right — rather than left — shoulder. Storm King looms just as majestically, and Mt. Beacon still towers across the way, but other mountains and another bridge beckon the gaze north instead of drawing one's attention south. From here, everything looks different.

To the north, apple farms being eaten up by suburbia still foster a rural atmosphere in contrast to Newburgh's urban ambience. Outlying small towns or villages struggle to preserve a sense of integrity while developers, capitalizing on the area's proximity to New York City, cater to commuters searching for a mini-castle surrounded by an immaculate lawn.

Every year, as spring's warmth melts into summer's heat, migrant farmworkers flood this area to harvest fruits and vegetables during the picking season. The entire Hudson Valley receives up to ten thousand temporary workers. Around twenty-five hundred harvesters come to this part of the valley to some fifty or more fruit and corn farms extended over an area of about 260 square miles. Known as a "stream," the eastern states (especially Florida, the Carolinas, and New York) host a migratory workforce that moves according to the seasons. Arriving in late June or early July, they work in the orchards until the end of October. At the corn camps, the season is even shorter, with workers staying for perhaps only six weeks or two months.

If one knows where to look from the ridges of certain country roads, small farmworker camps of trailers, wooden barracks, or cement block dormitories become visible. Forlorn during the better part of the year, for a few short months of picking season they come alive. One of the camps where my husband and I have *compadres* houses forty workers (the other half of the crew is spread out over several smaller farms). They turn the pasture between the dormitory and the apple trees into a soccer field; they fill the clothesline with hand-washed jeans and shirts; and they park two old school buses, one painted a flat, unconvincing white and the other aged to a dingy ochre, in the driveway. Even on picking days, there is usually someone around — unlucky stragglers suffering from the flu or the really unfortunate ones injured at work — besides the two cooks who sleep on a sofa in the dining room. Screen doors slam. Vehicles clamber along the dirt road. Music can be heard at any hour, its inevitable bass reverberating. It's the season.

Ordinary Time

The liturgical year has settled into the lull of summer, and the celebrant's emerald robes remind me of the lushness of our garden. The solstice has passed, and the chickens have reached their peak of egg-laying. With the children on school vacation, we enjoy a respite before the busy season of my husband's clinic begins. The church enters a new season: ordinary time.

Like the sudden outpouring of the Holy Spirit at Pentecost, my unexpected pregnancy with Seamus had overturned our lives more than we could have guessed possible. A six-month program I had initiated at work needed a new staff person, as its opening night just happened to coincide with my due date. Travel plans, already postponed for four years, had to be delayed some more. My energy level plummeted, with a summer cold lasting into December.

That year brought the worst drought in fifty years. The garden (an important supplement to our food budget) lay parched and neglected. Plants refused to thrive. Our few tomatoes were too small to be of much use. Greens wilted and shriveled. Cornstalks grew deceitfully tall; inside the husks, their ears failed to form kernels.

Exhausted by even the simplest household tasks, I found myself resenting my husband's job, work that he loved. Patience drained, I screamed at our children. Spending long hours near the river, walking or sitting on its banks, was the only way I found to soothe my ragged nerves. Finally summer cooled into autumn, and with winter's onset the birth grew closer.

Both of our older children came a week after their due dates; this birth came early. The only time in any of the three births it has happened, my water broke. As we drove over Storm King Mountain, going south on a clear noon in early January, I promised the child that we both would be born again that day. Crossing the bridge that separates the two sides of the Hudson Valley, I watched the sunlight dance on joyous waves and the wind sweep across the vast river's surface. By the time we arrived at the birth cottage, I could hardly wedge myself out of the back seat. Right away the midwife ushered me into the bathtub, surrounding the baby with his element. The midwife kept repeating, "Every contraction brings him closer to your arms." He was born after only two pushing contractions; he was as ready as I was.

It took me three times to get it right: to give my body over fully, to abandon myself completely to these children, to finally embrace this strange vocation of writer/mother/theologian, to dive deeply into this complex life I love. Watching the majestic river sparkle on that sunny day in early January, I promised to stop fighting and allow new life to flood through me. Now begins the hard work — the discipline — of relearning daily patterns.

At five months, Seamus grows like a weed. No longer does the soft spot on top of his head make me delirious with its milky baby smell. Messy mashed carrots or bananas smeared across his face replace our ecstatic nursing closeness. His poop begins to stink. Lullabies have given way to nap time in the car. My mother has stopped coming over on Thursdays while my husband works a late clinic night. I am slowly getting used to juggling the challenges of a new routine.

And so Seamus, gift of the Spirit and baptized on Pentecost, leads our family to the cusp of ordinary time. But this time, I promise myself, *this time,* I will cultivate the interiority that sustains me — and through me, all of us — in our family life. Like a gardener gingerly staking the thin stem of a fragile plant, I will tend to the ordinary that sheathes the extraordinary. Another chance has been given me, another chance to live as if *only one thing is necessary.* I pray for the discipline to be attentive to the flowing and outpouring of grace into our daily lives.

IN ANOTHER TOWN outside of Newburgh, over 150 years ago when mining provided the mainstay of the economy just south, a similar type of work camp attracted a different kind of immigrant. Irish men, most of whom had left their families back home, worked the mines and lived in roughly constructed barracks with scarce water and improvised sanitation. Cut off from the rest of the population by lack of transportation, they were looked down upon anyway by the town dwellers. Newburgh's archives record a Roman Catholic priest, the pastor of a parish in Highland Falls, responding to why he could not provide a Mass once a month to the thirty-five Catholic men in one mining camp.

First of all, he explained, the miners could not contribute enough from their meager wages to make his trip financially viable. Second, given the distance, he would have to stay overnight and there was no decent place to sleep in their overcrowded, filthy bunkhouses. Third, even overlooking the paltry remuneration and poor accommodations, the men would be too hung over from their Saturday night drinking to show up to the early morning Mass. He insisted that he was available for emergencies and that he did, at least, make the trip a few times a year; his assistant, on the other hand, refused to go there on any condition.

IN A CATHOLIC ACCOMPANIMENT PROJECT led by my husband's mentor, a Christian brother, our parish priest and a dynamic Mexican priest from a church across the river (among others) go out to the camps to say Mass. One year, we got to know don Celestino. A stalwart parishioner in his own hometown, don Celestino came from one of the nearby farms to attend. At middle age, he was older than the majority of the farmworkers, and he used his position as an elder to enforce proper behavior at Mass. Though he himself was a guest at this camp, he would turn to glare at the *muchachos* standing in the back to make sure they knelt at the appropriate moments. If they did not, he would hiss over his shoulder, *"de rodillas"* (kneel), and, chastened by his scowl, they would drop to their knees.

Don Celestino startled me during the first Mass of the season by another habit: at the moment of the elevation of the host, he broke the silence by declaring in a loud, unabashed voice, *"Señor mío y Dios mío."* The first time it happened, I felt slightly annoyed by the voice that had interrupted such an intimate moment. But others in the room were forgiving — even approving — of his call to focus their attention. After all, the Eucharist is neither a private event nor an individual one, but belongs to a whole community — a community in exile, marching on an exodus journey.

The travels of migrant farmworkers serve for me as a metaphor for the spiritual life. The most disenfranchised and powerless of this country's workforce, they embody a radical dependence on God. Constantly on the move, farmworkers cannot accumulate possessions: they must constantly prioritize what is essential and what is not. Shuttling between worlds, they may get lost between them — or they may discern how to carry one geography into another. Habits, idioms, and skills acquired in one place travel with them into the next.

Lacking in formal education, many farmworkers we have met possess agricultural and practical wisdom in abundance. They may not know how to read or write, but they value and internalize knowledge more deeply than I do. Often I am surprised by the accuracy of an illiterate person's memory. My husband warned me not to make proposals I did not intend to keep: a person's word is taken as bond, and country people regard as a promise what a city person considers simply a suggestion.

Country people are often reticent and sometimes distrustful of strangers, but once one has earned their trust, their friendship is earnest. Since migrants are so mobile, they may be easier to befriend than immigrants who are settled in insular pockets of their families and communities. Forced to depend on the kindness of strangers, they can be especially attuned to others' needs. Intense friendships among migrants from different states or even different countries of origin can develop. We have met fiercely loyal traveling companions who met only while crossing the border, or co-workers who live together and seem like family.

Ministry to farmworkers requires a spiritual wakefulness, a readiness to let go of the past and face the present with renewed fervor. Missing one season, one might return to the same farm the next year to find a whole new crew. Greeting old friends at the start of a season, one cannot assume anything; life has taken them places one cannot imagine. To befriend new arrivals, one must leave a controlled environment behind in order to meet them, literally, where they are. Migrants far from home, strangers in a foreign land, they become, nevertheless, hosts as they receive visitors at the camp.

While befriending newcomers on a one-on-one basis, one cannot lose sight of the fact that migrants carry a propensity for community, and that the circumstances of their lives will inevitably force a shifting and reshaping of that community. My husband or I may meet someone briefly, in one highly charged encounter that both will remember for the rest of their lives — and never see each other again. Or one can build friendships year after year that may deepen into *compadrazgos* when a baby is baptized, a teenager confirmed. Only after building *confianza* (trust) did farmworkers start asking my husband to translate for them and their employers, asking favors or making complaints.

The precariousness of migrants travels with them — especially for those here illegally. They cannot be "saved" by outsiders, only helped or befriended on a temporary basis. No matter how much one does to respond to their needs, one is barely scratching the surface. After a couple of years had passed — and after we became *comadres* — the mother of one family shared with me how much her youngest son had suffered, entering school as the class's only Latino, without a word of English. They had been too shy to ask for help, and I had not known enough yet to realize how much of a difference such a simple neighborly gesture would have made.

After my husband did special favors for families, I learned to anticipate a huge bag of apples, a home-cooked dish, or a hand-embroidered *servilleta* filled with homemade *tortillas* the next day. I was puzzled once by a woman's reaction when I went to drop off Christmas presents for her two children (we had forty or so toys donated through the parish). Her stony face and strangely stiff manner made me question whether my gesture had overstepped the bounds of etiquette. It was only when she rang our doorbell the day *after* Christmas, bearing presents for each of our children, that I understood. She did not consider ours a one-sided philanthropy but a reciprocal relationship, closer to a friendship. In friendship, repayment may not be equal, but must be mutual.

Farmworkers are not less apt to abuse alcohol, or take advantage of each other, or fall into domestic violence than the rest of us. Their lives are like all of our lives, but thrown into sharp relief, forced to live in the present moment. Their failings too magnify our failings: isolation, broken families, alcoholism, and exploitation. But like the rest of us, given the transient, liminal state of our lives, when they show living examples of moral courage and selfless compassion, one is graced with a glimpse of revelation.

Corpus Christi

When my six-month-old son eats, he *eats*. The biggest of our three children, he demonstrates a demanding appetite. During pregnancy I could hardly take in enough nutrition, and after birth, breast-feeding every couple of hours barely seemed to stay his hunger. I started him on rice cereal mixed with my milk at only four months. Applesauce followed soon after. Now bananas, squash, and carrots are adventures worthy of his full attention. Hearing his big sister sing in the next room or the rooster crow outside the kitchen window, he averts his head, refusing the spoon until his focus has returned to the act of eating.

How appropriate that the feast of Corpus Christi falls during ordinary time: an invitation to pay attention in the midst of our regular busyness. A chance to grasp once more at the golden thread that gets lost in the labyrinth of our daily lives.

Daily life never stops. There are children to be cared for, fed, clothed; a weekly antiwar vigil to be attended; a house to be cleaned and a garden to be weeded; plans to be made for parish and Grail programs. "Extras" come up with unpredictable immediacy: on a Sunday morning the doorbell rings and don Enrique is here for help translating immigration paperwork. But it is only since having children that I have started going to daily Mass. Attention divided by the simultaneous antics of a kindergartner, a preschooler, and a baby, I crave those quiet minutes when, like a Zen koan, the Eucharist snaps my mind into a single, brief recognition.

Depending on the homilist, sermons can be banal. When there is music, it is usually atrocious; the sexist language, always irritating. But inevitably some vital message surfaces in the Liturgy of the Word. As the celebrant prepares the gifts, my mind begins to settle down. Thoughts drift to the needs I can and cannot fill. My husband will be working at the farmworker clinic today; our children will need all my patience. The mother of a friend is gravely sick in Mexico. One of the apple-packing warehouses burned down and a *comadre* is out of work. There is the women's group and a catechism class to prepare — how can I make them interesting? Our daughter needs more outlets for her creativity. Laying out my worries, unconsciously I begin to distinguish between those I can affect and those that can only be given up to prayer.

Then, with the words I love — "Blessed are you, Lord God of all creation . . . fruit of the vine and work of human hands" — a shift happens. I think of our garden bursting at the seams; fat, beautiful baby Seamus in the bathtub; the Hudson River at the foot of Storm King Mountain. Daily work no longer seems futile. Grace feels not only possible, but imminent. I recognize the single thread that pulls me inward as the same one that ties together my multiple daily commitments.

And then come the words that rivet my being: "This is my body. This is my blood." In sharp relief, a single focal point shines. The white disc and then the gleaming chalice are held up for just a couple of seconds, and in those seconds, something in me whispers, Here. Look here. With all my heart and mind and soul, as if for the first time, I pay attention.

Seamus's perfect body grows heavier by the day. Mass over, I come home and we settle into the rocking chair for his afternoon nap. As with my two other children, I plan to breast-feed him, even as he begins solid food, until we are both ready to stop. Thomas may be emptying the chicken feed into the bathtub, and Rachel may be trying on my best tablecloth for dress-up. But with skin-on-skin contact and the baby's rosy lips fastened, nursing hormones kick in. Even here, in this postindustrial city of Newburgh, mindful of our ongoing wars in Iraq and other places, even with the hectic pace of a "simple" lifestyle, my hopes for a world at peace are restored. Blond eyelashes against his cheek, Seamus drifts to sleep wearing the face of satisfied desire.

I had watched those eyelashes come in. At first nonexistent, they made their appearance as two slight, shining lines parallel to his slowly darkening eyebrows. Growing more visible in gradations over the months, then extending longer, they finally curled upward in a golden arc.

The Psalmist sings, "I have calmed and quieted my soul like a child nursed at its mother's breast" (131:2). Fully attentive, fed by the Body of Christ, I nourish other lives. My own hunger satisfied, like a child nursed at her mother's breast, I am present; I am at prayer. The golden thread runs through my body, held loosely in his half-closed fists.

WHEN WE BRING A PRIEST out during the season to say an evening Mass for the crew and others from nearby farms, the night follows a certain pattern. The priest arrives as the workers themselves had arrived — carrying his belongings in a backpack. A missalette, hosts and wine, a small altar cloth, and vestments are all he needs. We wait for latecomers. My husband checks up on patients who have recently gone to the clinic. Our children run around on the grass. As I distribute the song sheets, even my *compadre* and others who can't read take them to look at the pictures.

At the cusp of summer, the lingering sun sheds a thin shell of light over the solid concrete block dormitory, casting shadows oblong and sharp. The mountain against which the camp huddles rises above us. If it is already autumn, the arms of apple trees darken sharply in the late afternoon like scrimshaw patterns carved into the background. Rows and rows of orchards run up and down the hills, their regularity relieved by undulating curves that hint at more orchards, hidden from view. Inside the mess hall, lockers line one side of the room, and a bulletin board full of posted information about workers' rights lines the other. Glaring lights burn overhead in the adjoining drab kitchen, whose stove is constantly in use and whose floor is always damp. The sink's perpetual drip piddles in the background. Floors filthied daily by forty men have been mopped and the tables moved out, into the kitchen. The picnic benches the men sit on during meals become the pews of this house church.

One of the cook's hand-embroidered cloths, with glossy red, orange, blue, and green threads stitched into patterns, transforms a picnic table into an altar. Wildflowers (usually the purple looses-trife that has taken over the wetlands) adorn the altar, set before an image of the Virgin of Guadalupe. The Mass is about to begin. The Christian Brother who has been Kenney's mentor these seven years slips unobtrusively into the crowd. Our children sit with the children in this crew, whom we visit season after season. *Mucha-chos* wearing sheepish expressions — suddenly reminded of the deeply ingrained *respeto* they thought they left behind with their parents in their villages — take off their baseball caps.

Musicians from the crew plunk out their favorite songs to the Virgin of Guadalupe on the guitar. Faces change, but always there are at least two or three from their number to lead music. My husband has taken pains to identify the few in the group who can read, and from among them, someone who can read well (without *too* much embarrassment) in front of the crowd. In the prayers just before the consecration, the priest praises the God of all Creation and asks God to bless the bread and wine — fruit of the earth and product of farmworkers' hands.

This gathered group incarnates the Body of Christ on the move. They have made it against all odds to this gray dormitory, to this drab mess hall, and their work is what is being praised. This assembly too must find its way into the future as the Body of Christ. Travelling from Florida to the Carolinas to New York, only to begin the exodus march all over again, they must make peace with one another.

In some way, my little family's own journey has merged, mo-mentarily, with theirs. Kneeling on the hard, severe concrete floor, my gaze is directed to the host uplifted in the priest's hand. My husband kneels at my side; I feel the warmth of his arm, so close to mine. Our children fidget and whisper. When the host is raised, a shudder passes through the kneeling crowd. Only a few of us will receive communion, but the whole assembly strains toward this moment: a rustle of bodies shifting, a single, drawn-in breath, a suspended step in a never-ending, weary procession whose march will seem lighter after this celebration. Inevitably, I remember don Celestino's uttered words, "My Lord and my God." I know suddenly, with unquestionable surety, *this is the life I am supposed to be living*.

In the kitchen, stacks of soda and potato chips wait in a heap; my *comadre* and her daughters will help distribute them afterward. The men will tell my husband how far along they are with the harvest at the six or so different farms this crew works while we women will fuss over the rambunctious, soda-guzzling children. The glow of the upraised host and the echo of don Celestino's words will linger in my mind's eye for days.

> *On this mountain the Lord of hosts will make for all peoples*
> *a feast of rich food, a feast of well-aged wines. . . .*
> *And God will destroy on this mountain*
> *the shroud that is cast over all peoples,*
> *the sheet that is spread over all nations;*
> *God will swallow up death forever.*
>
> — *Isaiah 25*

A Mother's Divine Office

Motherhood is monastic. Walking into Gethsemani Abbey during Night Prayer, I had to catch my breath. Not one to be swept up by hero worship, even of such a worthy figure as Thomas Merton (or for that matter, Kathleen Norris), I had braced myself to be critical. Nevertheless, entering the chapel vault seated within this gentle fortress on the hill, I was overpowered by a sudden visceral reaction. As I watched the evening light pour in and listened to the monks' plaintive chant, I found myself thinking, "So this is what it looks like."

In Kentucky for a Grail meeting, I was far from home but not alone. Too young to be left behind with my husband and our two older children, five-month-old Seamus weighed heavy in my arms. We had spent an uncomfortable night in a new bed and an exhausting day in meetings. Sheer doggedness was the only thing keeping me awake. Wits scattered by what a friend only half-jokingly refers to as "milk-brain," I was familiar with this effort to remain watchful.

I found it easy to identify with the no-nonsense robes and hairstyles of the two rows of monks. My body's beauty has been sacrificed three times, and while its contours were only temporarily reshaped, its flesh remains permanently creased. After each pregnancy, inevitably some of my hair falls out, leaving me with a mother's tonsure: a ponytail that thins (even as my hips widen) with each child.

And I too have had to learn detachment from career ambitions and material possessions. My best jacket, treasured for some future teaching job, was ruined by milk stains; my grandmother's lace tablecloth shredded by my son Thomas's scissors.

But the shock of familiarity that made my stomach clench and deflated my lungs came from a recognition even more fundamental. Like a cave hewn into mountain rock, the chapel vault confronts the eye with relentless simplicity. A wooden cross dominates the space. An icon, the only ornament, graces otherwise bare walls. Windows stretching several stories high allow natural light to ebb and flow. I found myself staring at a visual portrait of the *kenosis*, the self-emptying, brought about by this last, unexpected pregnancy.

My husband and I thought we had mastered the balance of work and family, even amid the chaos of our Catholic Worker lifestyle. Having two children already, we assumed that with minor adjustments (like finding health care coverage) our parameters would remain basically the same. This time was different. My energy level plummeted. I waited for the middle semester "second wind." It never came. Checkups, prenatal vitamins, and daily exercise, par for the course in my other pregnancies, became accomplishments in themselves.

As my husband and I began to pare down our active lives, we were forced to admit we had been doing all the right things for all the wrong reasons. Trading off the kids while we raced around to migrant farmworker camps, the Grail Women's Center, or our inner-city parish, we had lost track of the source of our motivation — or, to use an old-fashioned word, our "vocation."

During this third pregnancy, taking in too much at one time became overwhelming; clutter became unbearable. I craved simpler foods. Our new limits dictated a simpler pace of life. My already slim work hours vanished into a leave of absence. We had to end our only formal project, a gardening program with Latino teenagers. While this new life took shape inside my body, pushing for room, I felt my outward life slipping away.

Even the Mass was as if taken away from me. In the first trimester, a tide of revulsion made it impossible to stomach the liturgy's sexist language. As the surge of anger subsided into the more usual annoyance, no matter how hard I tried I could not return to three-times-a-week attendance. Just as the noon bells chimed, the phone would ring with a complicated need, or an unexpected guest would arrive. I thirsted for the wine's sweet, burning sensation to seep into my chest. I hungered for the host to cleave to the roof of my mouth. Instead, my hunger and thirst were sharpened.

Deprived of the anchor that grounds my busy days, I groped for a lifeline. During stolen moments while Rachel and Thomas napped, I sat with the breviary my mother had so wisely given me when I left home. Savoring their poetry, I pored over the psalms, rediscovering the lines that had already saved me once, during my college crisis of faith. Stitching each word into memory, I marvelled at the way they, in turn, baste my own small story into the seam of Christian history. I thought of those early communities of women and men who fled the comfort of urban center and the security of Constantine's church. They too were haunted by this desire: "I will lure you into the desert and there I will speak to your heart" (Hosea 2:4).

At thirty-three, I am the inheritor of two great lay movements, both of which must be reborn into the present generation. As mother of three, I can labor for neither one. Following a calling that demands so much from me, I had been faithful to its appearances while resisting its internal giving over. As their externals were stripped away, I found myself face to face with the original imprint on which the Catholic Worker and the Grail were based: the mystery of vocation laid bare. As in labor there is no going around the pain, only through it; and just as at Seamus's birth I had allowed the contractions to bowl me over, keeping nothing back from their agonizing waves, so now I allowed myself to be overwhelmed by the familiarity of this chapel.

Compline ended. All but one of the monks filed out. Invited to the inner chapel with the other visitors, Seamus and I lined up to be blessed with holy water. Passing the icon, we were greeted by the gaze of the Madonna holding her child. I thought of all those nights staying up with the children when they have fevers, watching their breath rise and fall in the O Antiphon of sleep. Motherhood is an office that, like dishes, or meals or countless miniscule acts of hospitality, must be re-created every day, several times a day.

At Gethsemani I recognized the tenacious return. Body exhausted, hair falling out, bound to late-night vigils and early morning lauds, I come back to the Liturgy of the Hours, to its words etched onto the bones. Like the monastics, I take my place in this remnant: to lean, fully awake, into stillness, embracing it like a lover; to seek the original imprint; to train an inner ear to the intimate voice of Christ.

Adoration

Kenney and I usually take Friday mornings as a couple. With our two older children in school and the baby captive in a backpack, we are suddenly blinded by the reprieve in our schedule and the rare luxury of time (almost) alone. But today, at the end of a long week, nerves raw from the demands of living with young children and worn out by the small defeats of this life we have chosen, we are in no mood to be together. We go for separate walks, he to scavenge the second-hand stores for a much-needed pair of shoes and I to watch the autumn fog sit heavy over the mountains. Still brooding, I slip into the back of the church. To my surprise, I find I am not alone.

On one side sits an elderly couple whom I often see at Mass. They stand out among others because of their habit of receiving communion side by side, instead of lining up properly with the rest of us. On the other side is another regular at daily Mass, a gentleman in his late fifties with an air of loneliness about him, who walks with a worsening limp. As I choose a pew, the silence already loosening the knots of anger in my back, my resentment begins to slip away. My eyes adjust to the dim light and I realize that the Blessed Sacrament is displayed on the altar. I had forgotten it was First Friday. What I did remember, as I sat in the comforting darkness, was that the sacramental sign for marriage is the Eucharist.

I have always been struck by how at the moment of consecration the host, a perfect, unblemished sphere raised in the hands of the celebrant, glows in completeness. A thing of beauty suspended in time and space, it glows, set apart from the rest of the world. Its unbroken circle, a unity of crushed grains baked into a single bread, reminds us of that eschatological promise that all will be one. But just as two thousand years ago Christ's body was crucified, at the moment of communion the perfect body must be broken: cracked, rent, torn, split, handed out in pieces so that its splinters of holiness can be consumed, consecrating our imperfect lives from the inside out.

Ten years ago, our love was perfect: insular, romantic, triumphant. Now our love is fragmented, divided first among our three children. Their bodies, like fragile wafers, bear the stamp of an original imprint beyond our design. Yet it is our love, spilled out and crushed like wheat, that procreated them. Given out completely, it is replenished when we come together in spite of ourselves. A multiplication of grace explodes in passion born out in a myriad of ways. Even in our imperfection and blindness, we must grope toward each other for our wholeness. In the braille of our marriage, we learn an intimacy that we can then sign to others.

I remember watching my husband with our second child. In my typical way, I had thrown myself into motherhood with Rachel, who kept us up with colic for three months and with teething for the next six. By the time Thomas came along, I was tired of night duty. Most nights Kenney kept vigil with our son. During those nights, a tenderness was awakened in him. I glimpsed that tenderness recently after a Mass at the camp. Kenney had made a special effort to invite a worker from another farm, a clinic patient whom he had recently taken to an emergency psychiatric visit. Despondent on hearing that his wife had given up on their marriage, Serafino lapsed into a depression that his friends feared could be suicidal. He wept as he explained that his wife had tired of waiting for him. She left his mother's house, taking their young son with her and leaving no word as to where she could be reached.

Dropping him off at the dormitory in the apple orchards, we waited in the car with the engine running as Serafino, listless, made no move to open the door. My husband leaned over the weathered seat and looked intently into Serafino's face for a moment. "Trata de descansar" (Try to get some rest), he said softly. "Sí, Kenney," Serafino replied wearily, unconvinced. They sat together in silence for a few more minutes while I watched from the back seat, where our three children lay asleep across my lap. Stunned, I had a flashback to the sight of my husband crooning to our son as he cradled the baby's body along his strong forearm at night, rocking his own body to put Thomas to sleep. "Sí, Kenney," Serafino replied again, this time more energetically, as he slowly got out of the car.

This is how Christ comes to us: with complete tenderness in broken shards. As my eyes adjust to the darkness of the church on this First Friday morning, I can only imagine all that the elderly couple has gone through in the history of their marriage. I can only guess at the loneliness of the man who, like Serafino, sits alone. Leaving the church to find my husband and take advantage of our remaining hour together, I genuflect before the Blessed Sacrament, bound and determined to work out my salvation.

Sent Forth

Farming and migrant farmwork, ironically, stand in diametric opposition. Farming is about staying on the land (usually land inherited from generation to generation), maintaining and improving the family's property in a basically conservative way of life designed to ensure stability, an integrated local economy, and family cooperation. Migrant farmworkers — most of them displaced from their own land — live an opposite way of life: moving from place to place, isolated from the local communities where they work, uprooted from the land of their birth and separated from their family members.

A small number of farmworkers stay on during the year to prune trees or to work in packing houses (warehouses where fruit is stored and packaged). Many of those employed in the packing houses actually live in Newburgh or one of the other surrounding towns, not on the farms. Packing is not as well paid as harvesting (an experienced picker can earn twice as much a day in the orchards than in the packing house), but it does offer the chance to stay year-round instead of moving with the seasons.

Those who "settle out" of the stream follow a similar pattern. First, they usually buy a car, which allows them to come and go as they please. If they are fortunate enough to work for a sympathetic boss and to be given decent housing, they may choose to remain on the farm. There are those who settle out but prefer the rural environment, like Luanne's ex-husband, a migrant from Florida who has lived in the country all his life. Others take an apartment, instead, in Newburgh or wherever they find cheap housing. Living off of the farm, they must pay not only rent but also transportation.

Eventually they move on to another kind of work, such as factory or service jobs.

It lasts longer than picking, but packing is not always stable work; often the job slows down (*se enfloja*) during late winter once the apple crop has been sold — or when fresh apples from other areas of the world appeal to consumers' palates more than the previous season's ones from local farms. Farming is risky business, especially for smaller family farms. Each year growers exchange gossip on who's getting out of the business. To finance the up-coming year's harvest many sell off parcels of their orchards for the subdivisions that are turning farmland into suburbs. But for the farmworkers, precariousness is lived at closer range. Once the crop has been brought in, the work ends. As fall turns toward winter, the crews will have to return south, where they will seek work in Florida's orange groves.

EVERY YEAR as the season is about to end, rumors start as to when our *compadres'* crew will leave. Though a contract has been signed with the grower extending until the end of the month, everyone knows that the end of the harvest cannot be regulated by a calendar. Different kinds of apples are picked at different times, and depending on the severity of the ensuing frosts, the size of the crew, and the peculiarities of a given year, the harvest is done when it is done. The crew leader himself does not know when they will leave.

But by some time in late October, the word has been given and a sudden crunch of packing, cleaning, and closing up for the year begins. There is no work that day, nor the next — the day of departure — and so the men stand around, their backpacks stuffed, their mood jovial. Those who have bought stereos or bikes at yard sales have loaded them onto a wheeled camper. The two school buses fill with bodies. Those who have their own cars will follow in a caravan.

Despite the cold (by now the weather has inevitably changed), there is an air of excitement. Wearing their cleanest clothes, the men look ready for a special occasion. The *penosos* (timid) who never before gave anything more than a minimal greeting suddenly make conversation. Addresses are left by those with whom one has wittingly — or unwittingly — established a connection. (Sometimes I am surprised by who chooses to scrawl their directions on a scrap of paper with the injunction that, if we make it to Mexico, we must come and visit.) If a stray stereo is not yet packed up, there is music blasting. The weather will be warmer in Florida, and a new season brings new possibilities. Some of the men will be returning home for Christmas, and so this may be good-bye.

Partings are bittersweet, but there is an unmistakable glee: what one is going *to* may prove to turn out better than what one is leaving *behind*. My *compadres* try to hide their excitement, showing a proper deferential sadness in order not to make us feel bad, but I can tell by the glint in their eyes that they are glad to move on. As the men pile onto the bus, joking as they jostle for space, we catch a glimpse of their indomitable spirit. Their optimism is palpable.

"MISSA," from which our word "Mass" is derived, means, literally, "sent forth." We have put down roots in Newburgh, but our spirits long to fly with the freedom of migrant wings. Joined in marriage and strengthened by the Eucharist, my husband and I, at picnic table altars covered with delicately embroidered cloths, catch a glimpse of our vocation's fullness ripening in the apple orchards.

** *Eight* **

Restoration

The crows descend each evening in our backyard. Scores of them with slate-colored wings and compact bodies swoop in from wherever they go during the day, settling in for a winter's night. Each claims a spot along a tree branch's rough arm for the evening cacophony. Mornings at five o'clock, again they squawk their ungainly chorus from the half-dead tree whose branches, my husband fears, will one day crash onto our neighbor's roof.

Having lived in that one house for more years than I have been alive, our neighbor, Sam, has watched this city from a single vantage point for more than five decades. His unmarked storefront takes in dry cleaning and feeds every stray cat in the neighborhood. A couple of years ago, Sam noticed the birds moving in to roost at night. "I've never seen so many crows before," he exclaimed. "Where do they all come from?"

At certain times of the year, the crows are joined by smaller, less conspicuous feathered relatives. No grace in them, they forgo fancy flight patterns and fly, pragmatic, not for the joy of it but to tackle the matter at hand: making a space for themselves among the crows. These migratory birds, known by an ungainly name, grackles, added a new word to my vocabulary.

THE RIVER AND THE PEOPLES along these banks have been known by different names. The Mohawks called themselves "People of the Place of Flint," since the word "Mohawk," conferred upon them by their enemies, actually meant "Those Who Eat People." Similarly, the word "Iroquois" comes from a slur originating with their rivals, the Algonquins, who deprecatingly named them "The Adders."

The Five Nations (Mohawks, Oneidas, Senecas, Onandagas, and Cayugas) were more properly known as "The People of the Long House" for their distinctive homesteads.

Like the Five Nations people, the Algonquins, who came from the west around 1300 C.E., were actually a group composed of several tribes. Named for animals, such as the Wolf or the Turtle, tribes joined in alliances for intermarriage and protection. At the time of the Europeans' arrival, the Lenape Alliance dominated this bank of the river. The present-day names of many towns, rivers, streets, and mountains are derived from their names — the Delaware, the Wappinger, the Manhattans, the Tappans, the Hackensacks, or Haverstroos.

The river too has been called by many names. The Mohawks called it "Beautiful River," while to other tribes it was "The River That Flows Both Ways." Henry Hudson called it "The River of the Mountains" — never suspecting that it would someday bear his own name. The Portuguese and Spanish, thanks to Gomez's expedition, depicted it on their maps as the "Río San Antonio," or, in the explorer's honor, "Río de Gomez." Just previously, Verrazano had named it the "Río Grande." For English speakers, officially the Hudson was "The Mauritius," but popularly it was dubbed "North River" (as opposed to the "South River," the Delaware).

Even ice had its own vocabulary, popularized during the one hundred or so years of ice harvesting when depots along the river cut, stored, and shipped ice to New York City. "Fast ice" is ice attached to the bottom of the river or to the shore, while "drift ice" floats, unattached. An expanse of ice must measure at least fifty yards wide to be a "field," while a "floe" measures between ten and fifty yards. "Brash" is ice in small fragments. "Slusk" is an accumulation of crystals. When broken ice is pressed haphazardly into mounds, it is "hummocked." When pushed into constricted areas, it is "jammed."

RECENT NEWCOMERS to the Hudson Valley bear many names. Among Spanish speakers, each country (and within each country, each region or state) has its own nicknames. Some are understood as offensive while others are not. For example, from an indigenous word for stranger in a foreign land, *chilangos* (from the nahuatl *chilangotl*) designates people from Mexico City. Known to be quick and clever, they often have European blood and tend to look down on their more indigenous counterparts. When used by someone from the *provincia*, the term *chilango* is understood to mean a city person who lords it over (or, takes advantage of) humbler *paisanos* recently arrived from the countryside.

To English speakers, however, Latinos or Hispanics are unconsciously perceived as "all the same." Like our neighbor who does not distinguish between crows and grackles, the Census lumped all South Americans into one category — though the differences between European-identified, cosmopolitan Argentines with their distinctive language and indigenous-influenced Peruvians from remote Andean villages seem obvious.

To Latinos, Caucasians are *blancos* (whites) or *gabachos*, from the derogatory word used for the Spanish by Latin Americans. Mexicans will often call whites *güeros* and nickname the lighter-complected among themselves *güeros* or *güeras*. *Gabacho* or *gabacha*, however, is strictly reserved for non-Latinos. A more playful term employed with some frequency is *bolillo*, a white bread that is crusty on the outside and soft on the inside.

The most offensive term for whites is *gringo*, or in Central American parlance, *yanqui*. Sometimes I have found in talking with Latinos who did not yet realize that I am a *bolilla* (people sometimes mistake me for a *chilanga*), they spoke of whites as *gringos*. Once they realized their mistake, most often — in deference to my sensibilities as a *gabacha* — they more politely referred to my people as that worst of misnomers, *americanos*. African-Americans, Asian-Americans, Native Americans, and U.S.-born Latinos are all "American," too, though not white. In Nicaragua, when I replied *americana* to the question of my nationality, I was severely corrected: "We are all Americans." In Latin America, schoolchildren are taught that North, South, and Central America together compose one continent. Thus, all its inhabitants are Americans.

When the Mexica nomadic tribe wandered to central Mexico, looking for the sign given to them by the gods as to where they should settle, they traveled in the desert until they came upon an eagle sitting atop a cactus, eating a serpent. The name *chilango* was given to them by the settled people amid whom they found themselves. In the Judeo-Christian telling of a similar story, it was only after the deportation, during the Exile, that the Israelites in captivity came to be known for the first time as "Jews." Derived from the word "Judah," which in actuality referred to only the Southern Kingdom and to only one of the twelve tribes, the term originated with their captors, the Babylonians.

Understood in its original indigenous meaning, Newburgh is full of *chilangos* — foreigners who have come from somewhere else to find themselves outsiders in another's land. Even whites in Newburgh, who number in the minority, can be considered as *chilangos*. It is, perhaps, our only authentic common identity: sojourners wandering between exodus and exile on the banks of the Hudson River.

IN SUMMER, music of numerous varieties drowns out the sound of birds on the city's streets. The Hondurans in the mechanic shop bordering our lower garden prefer music of tropical variety, such as *salsa, merengue*, or the lively *punta* (a Honduran trademark). Our Mexican neighbors upstairs elect, rather, swooning *ranchera* or upbeat (and atonal) *banda* music; involved *corridos* tell border-crossing stories and exaggeratedly romantic ballads that would melt any lover's heart unravel tales of loyalty or betrayal.

The kids on the street, of course, have ears only for rap. At family barbecues held on the other side of the block, however, oldies prevail. Whoever takes charge of the music holds the same tastes as the older generation from the South in the Heights. I stand transfixed on our back patio on Sunday afternoons, listening to the voices of my childhood: seventies music that crosses from disco to soul to funk — many songs of which I had played over and over on my 45 records during the time of my exile.

Renaissance

Arise, shine; for your light has come,
  and the glory of the Lord has risen upon you.
For darkness shall cover the earth,
  and thick darkness the peoples;
but the Lord will arise upon you,
  and God's glory will appear over you.
Nations shall come to your light,
  and rulers to the brightness of your dawn.

Lift up your eyes and look around;
  they all gather together, they come to you;
your sons shall come from far away,
  and your daughters shall be carried on their nurses' arms.
Then you shall see and be radiant;
  your heart shall thrill and rejoice,
because the abundance of the sea shall be brought to you,
  the wealth of the nations shall come to you.

— *Isaiah 60*

The words of the third prophet Isaiah, from the last of the book's three sections, were written for a people coming out of exile. The Jews in captivity (and in the Dispersion) hoped that their dream of resettling in their own land might be fulfilled. The Babylonian empire had fallen to Cyrus of Persia, and the horizon of their homeland seemed attainable for the first time since the deportations. After a full generation of despair, the prophet's words were meant to give instruction and encouragement. If Judah were restored from exile, Isaiah reminds his hearers, it must again serve as a light to all nations.

The passages in Third Isaiah place Israel's history within cosmology. If the people were brought home, it would be thanks to God's mercy; they must, then, acknowledge God's everlasting plan for creation. All nations are the context for God's redemption. Even nature will be renewed. Through the restoration of

175

a single, particular people, all of the world — indeed, all of the universe — will be enlightened.

The promise given to Abraham will blossom with a yield abundant enough to extend to all peoples. A new creation is coming, so close that it can be glimpsed on the horizon. But the best news is that the new heavens and new earth so longed for are *home*. Restoration means a homecoming to our own lands that we thought had been lost forever. Expecting to find the countryside wasted and infertile — or dreading to see the city of our dreams ruined and sacked as it had been when we had left it in chains — we will arrive to find our homeland re-created, better than ever.

JUST AROUND THE TIME that my husband and I moved into Newburgh, the city plunged into urban revival plans. Publicists came up with the slogan "The Newburgh Renaissance," and developers (mostly from New York City) were invited to renovate property in the most distressed parts of the city. Capitalizing on Newburgh's unarguable wealth in architecture, with mansions and public buildings still bearing their former glory, the idea was that by giving the city's existing infrastructure a facelift, new homeowners and new businesses would be attracted to move in. Municipal buildings such as the city hall and the social services building were artfully renovated.

A building on the corner of our street was restored by one renovation company. For several months, workers sanded its impressive brick walls, replaced the wood detail that runs along its facade, put in new windows similar to the style of the old ones, and trimmed the exterior in contrasting colors. Once an abandoned, decrepit building (uninhabited for as long as I have known it), it now looks gorgeous — from the outside. Over a year later, and the space has been neither rented nor sold. Looking inside one sees that the interior space remains gutted and untouched. Painstakingly restored on the outside, on the inside the building is still an abandoned piece of property.

Along the river at the foot of Broadway where cattle used to be herded toward the water's edge, a new development was built as the centerpiece of the Newburgh Renaissance. Taking advantage of the waterfront location, a row of fancy restaurants offer diners the chance not only to enjoy the scenic panorama but to "be seen" in its upscale ambience. The development brings in much-needed revenues in tax dollars to the city. Priced too high for most city folks to afford, the restaurants attract, instead, diners from the suburbs. It hires city residents as dishwashers or as cleaners, but wait staff must be sophisticated enough to pronounce the fancy items on the menu.

Like a Third World vacation spot that draws tourists to elite enclaves without exposing them to local poverty, the new development belongs to a separate reality. A busy thoroughfare divides the waterfront from the rest of the city, with the restaurants on one side and the housing projects on the other. Driving in, one can avoid Broadway altogether: the string of restaurants is accessible from a river road leading in from the surrounding suburbs. A wide expanse of abandoned land, now grown over with meadow, stands between the waterfront and the downtown. During the 1960s, the city razed several blocks of rental housing inhabited by working-class (mostly African-American) families. Contrary to politicians' promises, the neighborhood was never rebuilt.

In the meantime, family businesses along Broadway and in Newburgh's neighborhoods have popped up in an alternative kind of economic development. Grocery stores specializing in ethnic products, telephone and money-wiring *casetas*, barbershops, clothes stores and party shops, translation and paperwork services, numerous taxi companies, and restaurants have proliferated. The city now holds two *tortilla* factories.

The upscale restaurants on the waterfront may attract clientele from around the area, but so does the Mexican fast food eatery, "Los Tacos." Instead of a chilled salmon plate served with arugula salad, a Jamaican storefront restaurant sells spicy stewed goat. Farmworkers and other immigrants, whether Jamaican, Southern African-American, Central American, Mexican, or Bangladeshi, carpool or pay the expensive taxi fare to patronize these businesses. The locally owned establishments will soon have competition from a newcomer. A restaurant was just built on Broadway as the street's first franchise of a multinational corporation, whose fare, unfortunately, suits the budget — and tastes — of the city's residents: a McDonald's.

PETE SEEGER and the *Clearwater*'s campaign to clean up the Hudson River might be considered an early effort for the valley's restoration. All forms of life depend in some way on the health of the river's waters in a bioregion more interconnected and more delicate than residents of the valley had previously imagined. However, as the river was being cleaned of "traditional" pollutants, a more lethal but invisible type of pollution was poisoning its waters. Eighty-two million pounds of polychlorinated biphenyls (PCBs) were dumped into the river by General Electric plants, allowed to discharge up to thirty pounds a day. (The Department of Environmental Conservation would later be fined for its part in the desecration of the river's waters, with the penalties to go toward clean-up efforts.)

I remember when, in 1976, commercial fisheries were closed because of the PCBs, causing the collapse of an entire local trade. As a child, I remember the warnings not to eat fish caught in our beloved Hudson, but I also remember that our poor friends and neighbors, like Luanne's family and the men my brother and I came across at the creek, ate them anyway. The thought that an invisible pollutant more noxious than visible ones even then poisoned the river was sobering. In these environs, which felt like our home outdoors, I learned that the most poisonous dangers may be the ones that lurk below the surface.

JUST AS THE WATERFRONT was being renovated for the string of upscale restaurants that would regale its banks, an incident took place that shamed the city. A homeless African-American man lived along the water's edge in a van parked in one of the lots soon to be revamped. The man was by spotted by a roving band of four white teenage boys. Apparently offended by the sight of a homeless person, they set fire to his vehicle — with the man trapped inside. Hurt and traumatized but not critically injured, the man received medical attention and the boys were arrested. But the most shocking part of the story is that two of the teenagers are sons of the chief of police.

AFTER A GENERATION of captivity, and with numerous other families "settled out" in the Dispersion in surrounding countries, the return to Judah was fraught with difficulties. Jerusalem's struggles of reintegration are recorded in the books of Nehemiah and Ezra, and more poetically (although less explicitly) in the Song of Songs. Cyrus's empire, in unison with newly returned local religious and political leaders, would sanction the taxes to rebuild Jerusalem and its Temple. In what today would be seen as a gentrification campaign, the city's infrastructure would be rebuilt through the efforts of local religious and political authorities.

But those appointed to collect the taxes were confronted by a restless peasant populace. Those who had remained behind found themselves hard-pressed to suddenly supply cash (they had relied on a barter system). A drought had struck, and the farmland lay in famine. The peasants complained that their sons were being forced off the land into servitude, and their daughters into prostitution. They resented their recently returned countrymen who had assumed positions of control after a long absence. Restoration had to take place on a deeper level. Jerusalem would be reconstructed not by simply rebuilding its walls, but by reconciling her people.

A CROWD GATHERED for a housewarming on my old block. The organization Habitat for Humanity, which opened a chapter in Newburgh, had renovated its third house — all three in the neighborhood where I grew up. Recognizing that families who claim their own homes make more of an investment into the community than those who rent, Habitat concentrated on the Heights for its campaign of renovating dilapidated buildings. The organization's twin strategies of "sweat equity" and interest-free mortgages make homeownership possible for working-class families. Once fixed up, properties cannot be sold for a determinate length of time, thus avoiding land speculation and ensuring that families take their commitment to the neighborhood seriously.

Tomasa and Pedro, a couple from our church, stood at the top of the stairs — the day's honoraries. By the time of the housewarming, they had put in over double the hours required by Habitat's sweat equity policy. Their family was one of the first to come from Mexico to Newburgh. Now their youngest sons are teenagers themselves, growing up in the Heights.

The crowd gathered outside the steps leading up to a beautiful two-story brick house was made up of (mostly) white faces in this (mostly) African-American and Latino neighborhood. Many of them volunteers who pitched in to the renovation efforts, most came from the surrounding suburbs to neighborhoods they or their parents had left when waves of exodus bled the city's veins. I asked myself, scanning the sea of faces: truth to be told, when this housewarming ends, do I long to follow them somewhere else instead of *here?* To have my children grow up in a neighborhood where cars are not broken into and where windows are not randomly broken? Where passersby will not urinate on our front door, and where foul language or fights will not wake us up at night? Given the chance, perhaps I *would* abandon these streets, these neighbors, these memories, assigning them to the many junk stores of used-up cast-offs that line Broadway.

But underneath it all, I *do* long to save Newburgh. I cannot give up on these streets any more than I can erase the memorized landscape of river and mountains engraved on my heart. I have come to love these settlers and these migrants. Fascinated by Newburgh's archives, I have been even more enthralled by the newness of history in the making. One of the community's leading organizers, don Pedro campaigns for an amnesty for undocumented immigrants. Newburgh's restoration will never take place until its residents open their eyes to the exile around them and embrace the exodus journey that has led newcomers here. I pray for a true Renaissance, worthy of the name. I hope for Newburgh's true restoration. Rejuvenating the city from the inside out.

They shall build houses and inhabit them;
   they shall plant vineyards and eat their fruit.
They shall not build and another inhabit;
   they shall not plant and another eat;
for like the days of a tree shall the days of my people be,
   and my chosen shall long enjoy the work of their hands.
They shall not labor in vain,
   or bear children for calamity,
for they shall be offspring blessed by the Lord —
   and their descendants as well.

   — Isaiah 65

THE CROWS SETTLE for the night. Their beaks, pointed like quills, and tiny, sharp-clawed feet extend from plush, dark plumage. Sam and I comment in a neighborly way about these birds who have for some unknown reason chosen our small corner of the city. The grackles remain until late autumn, after other birds have already flown south in flocks. They return in early spring. For now only the crows remain, their coarse dark feathers like rats' fur resistant to cold, stubborn in their refusal to leave. Newburgh welcomes both migrants and settlers, crows and grackles.

SAM CLUCKS WITH EXASPERATION, "Renaissance! What Renaissance? I've heard it all before. Every fifteen years they come up with the same thing. They just give it a different name." Sam threatens every January to move to Arizona, and even puts a "For Sale" sign in his storefront window. My husband and I, *chilangos* like every other wanderer who has found a way to these banks, will make a home out of this city until the day we leave.

Trains

Surely they sound during the day, but somehow I hear the hollow, aching howl of the freight trains only at night. From a deep cavern of slumber, I emerge reluctantly, called from sleep as if to the mouth of a cave. I grope my way toward its beckoning call. It begins from far away, a flute-like ribbon issued from the engine's horn. Curling toward the city, it unfurls more and more rapidly as the locomotive's solid body hurtles closer. Several chords sound simultaneously, as if from the silver throat of a harmonica. With increased urgency, it rises into the air and floats above the cliff, over steeples and rooftops, until it finally bursts into a full roar over the sleeping city.

If these were the years of my childhood — and if this were daytime — my friends and I would have waited until just this precise moment to wave. We had timed it perfectly: our ragtag lineup would be visible at this split second to the locomotive driver. By the time the clamor of clacking train cars ascended over the cliff, the engine would already have moved on. The horn precedes the train's charging metal bodies. Lingering and plaintive, it puts listeners on guard, reminding them to keep a safe distance. Its function, after all, is to alert anyone and anything within hearing that coming too close could prove fatal. It is a sound imprinted in my memory since childhood. I cannot help but be roused from sleep.

ANOTHER EARLY MORNING BRAWL, and I awake to a heavy weight pressing on my chest. Doubt has replaced faith; a deep-seated panic rises to my throat. I have been attending Grail meetings all week with local women leaders from communities in Brazil, Mexico, and Honduras; perhaps that is why the sheer magnitude of evil overwhelms me more than a single altercation should. The Deceitful One skulks rampant through these streets — this world — and yet we go on with life as normal! Poverty in the developing world is deeper than it was twenty years ago, with more fiercely aggravated social problems. The hometown of the majority of Hondurans in Newburgh, a coastal city named San Pedro Sula, has taken the distinction of being the most violent city of any country in the Americas not currently embroiled in civil war.

What if it is a pious lie, this belief in redemptive suffering? What a laughable, ludicrous idea, that salvation could come through the obscure, insignificant death — the off-handed cruelty of which

I shudder to imagine — of a first-century carpenter belonging to an oppressed people in a conquered homeland! How could liberation come through his willingness to be hung on a cross, giving himself over to the very evil that still stalks a wounded humanity? Furthermore, how can a loving God work through us, given the miniscule scale and imperfect results of our efforts?

Like San Pedro Sula, Newburgh does not need to be at war for its residents to hear gunshots. Like those in Brazil's slums, our youth too willingly throw their lives away for drugs. And like those of Mexico, our farms have been deserted by our workforce: by necessity they are full of exiles from their own lands who have come to pick other growers' crops.

Newburgh is not the worst city I know of; it is definitely not the poorest. Anyone who has set foot in the developing world can tell the difference between two kinds of poverty. Even here, communities populated by those in exodus from the Third World profit from the exploitation of the Third World. We can buy manufactured goods made in sweatshops, and we enjoy a standard of living that, even though it may be substandard, does not come close to the abject poverty of developing countries. But Newburgh houses evil, too. It's just harder to get at.

WHEN AS CHILDREN we scrambled down the Bluff to enter the cool of the huge black tunnel or to lay coins to be flattened along the silver tracks, we luxuriated in the trains' power, with a concomitant sense of potential danger. We experienced a solidarity as we each risked our lives by grasping hands, plastered against the cool, sooty walls of the tunnel while engines with hot breath and metal bodies charged past our own weak, throbbing ones. We also, instinctively, grasped at our own freedom: the boys debated often where they should go if they ever got up the courage to "hop" a train (as they often boasted they would). The trains that could easily crush our young bodies could also transport us to places we could not yet imagine. The train's horn thrilled us, not only for its warning of danger, but for the freedom to which we would someday be entitled — our ticket out of here.

Saviors

In this city that so desperately needs saving, the simplest of gestures offered in good faith become sources of hope. Sometimes performed heroically for a stranger (e.g., the Good Samaritans who saved the young woman from assault), sometimes done quietly for one's own kin (e.g., Eduardo and his wife, who took in his cousin), they recall the works of mercy. Laura, whose family was so poor only a few years ago that she and her brother alternated donning one pair of shoes, frequently brings clothes or household furnishings to recently arrived women she meets at work. Other actions, more collective in scale (such as don Pedro's organizing for an amnesty) build upon these relationships. Developed and shared within the underground community itself, these alternative networks elude the institutions that have excluded immigrants. Few undocumented workers have bank accounts, for example, but most participate in a *tanda* (an informal rotating fund).

Our neighbor who worked as an elementary school teacher in Mexico now takes in other women's children for $40 a week. Her response to the need of working mothers with young children may be small, but her commitment to provide a loving, attentive environment at a just price is momentous. Another woman makes her business a place of hospitality. A middle-class Dominican who owns a *caseta*, she finds herself in a position to give *consejos* to recently arrived immigrants as to where to find jobs, housing, the soup kitchen, and (in winter) warmer clothes. Often she serves as a witness to the grief of those separated from their families: she hears them weep into the receiver during their weekly phone calls. Having been through her own share of health problems, immigration red tape, and marital difficulties, she gives her own testimony to anyone facing similar problems. When someone seems particularly troubled, she offers to help that person pray.

ALEYDA SITS EACH WEEK in church while her children attend catechism. A Salvadoran by birth, she is an undocumented farmworker who earns minimum wage packing apples. She and her family live in a two-room cottage on a farm outside Newburgh. Aleyda and her brothers came to this same farm as teenagers. She has not been home in fifteen years; she cannot leave without risk, since she is here illegally. Her children, born in Newburgh, have never met their maternal grandparents.

About eight years ago, Aleyda's youngest brother was shot and killed by police. It was a Sunday afternoon, she told me; he had gone out alone to do the week's grocery shopping. Stopped by officers at a roadblock nearby the farm, he panicked and fled. The other brothers on the farm remember hearing a ruckus of police sirens and screeching wheels, but they had no idea it was their brother who was in trouble. By the time they found out what had happened, someone was needed at the morgue to identify the body.

From what they understood (none of the family speaks English), police claimed that their brother had a criminal record and was under warrant for arrest for having killed a police officer in Houston. Aleyda and her brothers never knew for sure whether this was true. On the one hand, he *had* spent time in Houston apart from the family. On the other hand, he might have been confused under his *prestanombre* ("borrowed" name on false working papers) for someone charged with the crime. The fact that he had panicked when police checked his license indicated to them his guilt, but to other undocumented immigrants, who fear being caught with false identification, it seemed understandable. Yet another possibility is that Aleyda's brother panicked because in their country, during the bloody civil war during which they grew up, a single interrogation could be lethal.

Aleyda and her brothers never learned to read or write, since teachers in their rural zone were routinely disappeared or killed. For years the men of their village went out to sleep in the *bosque* (woods), afraid the army would massacre them in a night raid. Here in Newburgh, Aleyda is adamant that her children take catechism classes. Her kids — the most respectful, responsible, and personable adolescents I've ever met — show through their disciplined behavior the close watchfulness by which their mother has raised them. She waits for them to finish class, and then they take a cab home again. When her husband works nights, Aleyda and her kids take the half-hour taxi ride from the farm. The fare takes an entire day of her wages. When I see her sitting in the church, serene and prayerful, my own spirit lifts. Her gentle, determined face tells me that her children, at least, will be saved.

Roses

A teenage girl sits at the round dining room table of my child-hood. Just turned sixteen, Janet is pretty, with arching eyebrows and a regal face. Dressed in the latest style, she takes great care that her bell-bottom jeans (manufactured to look used), sneakers (name brand, of course), and unisex jacket (brightly colored but studiously plain in design) conform to the casual style that serves as a uniform for fashion-conscious teenagers.

Janet has come to me for a *consejo*. We had built up trust in my sixth-grade catechism class. But even more, I know her mother, father, sister, and brother. I know her numerous uncles and aunts, her tribe of cousins. Their family history goes back to the founding of a village in Morelos, Mexico, a *pueblo* Janet has never visited; Janet's great-grandfather fought alongside Emiliano Zapata. I know her uncle the *mariachi,* and her grandmother, who could explain to me what life was like in the *pueblo* better than any anthropologist's informant.

Janet could talk to any one of the grown-ups in the clan of her family, but she has chosen me instead. An outsider to her family's tight-knit community, I am an observer, not a participant. I can be trusted not to spread her confidence through *chisme* (gossip). In the family, important matters such as this one should be discussed through *padrinos;* her *padrinos,* however, live in Florida, and anyway, things are done differently here. Her parents have a right to be angry. After all, they came here, leaving everything they knew, for her. She is the reason they risked their lives crossing the border and then spent the last eight years, day in and day out, at low-paying jobs — her father getting up at four o'clock in the morning for his job at an apple-packing house and her mother ruining her knee in a factory injury.

And now, Janet is seven weeks pregnant. When I ask if she loves the father of the baby, she guesses that she *must* love him, "because you only have a baby with someone you love." Her boyfriend is willing to do the right thing and move her in with his ten relatives in a two-bedroom apartment. Will I help her break the news to her parents?

Janet has been to the new McDonald's on Broadway to fill out a job application and says she will call about G.E.D. classes. She cannot attend college anyway, since being here illegally, she would not be eligible for financial aid. She thinks she and her boyfriend will soon be able to rent their own apartment. In her eyes I see the unrealistic expectations of love and the future held by my childhood friends all over again. I recall Angelique, Ruby, and Marisol — none of whom I ever saw again, all of whom became pregnant at precisely this age. I say what I can to counsel her, but I know that her future choices — as well her past ones that led up to this moment — are beyond my control.

I know intimately the environment that acts as a backdrop for Janet's present predicament, as well as the loneliness, alienation, and unrealistic daydreams that set actions into play. I have not experienced the racism that leads young people like Janet to seek consolation in each other's arms, alienated from their families by the prejudice that denigrates their culture — or made hopeless about the future when they think that their lives will end up like their parents', toiling at jobs white people won't do. I *have* felt the urge to escape Newburgh's hopelessness. But the difference is, I did get out.

Returning here happily married with three beautiful (and very wanted) children, I grope for the words to address a situation I escaped. Janet comes from a cultural background that this society finds hard to understand, much less esteem. How can I convince her that her life is already worth more than she suspects? Watching Janet's expressive face, her thick, curved lips and beautifully molded features accentuated by the gold hoop earrings, I sit at the round kitchen table of my childhood and experience a sense of familiar grief.

It is like calling out to a train about to crash over a cliff, helpless to stop it. It is like watching a movie whose tragic ending you already know, but which you can't rewind or remake. It is like crying out from the Bluff's grassy edge to a sailboat gliding past when you are the only one who can see it is destined for the rocks, only to have your voice carried away by the wind that buffets the river's choppy waters.

> *God said to me, "You are my servant,*
>   *Israel, in whom I will be glorified."*
> *But I said, "I have labored in vain,*
>   *I have spent my strength for nothing and vanity;*
> *yet surely my cause is with the Lord,*
>   *and my reward is with my God."*
> — *Isaiah 49*

THE SUFFERING SERVANT images appear in the third grouping of the three prophets collectively known as Isaiah. To achieve the new creation described so gloriously in Isaiah's passages, sacrifice will be called for. Restoration will entail hard work, self-giving, and a willingness to leap into the new moment of God's love. A desert will flower; a wasteland will be brought back to life. The utopian vision is the destiny of Israel; but a *kenosis* on the part of God's suffering servant will be necessary to bring it about.

In order to experience the transformed homeland, one must let go of the old one. In order to reconcile returning exiles with those who stayed, bringing them together as one people, both sides have to bend. In order to be a light for the nations — light which originates not *from* any one people, but from God's love *for* them — God's people must first acknowledge their source of blessing. The Suffering Servant fulfills that function.

Emptying himself in order to orient them toward this truth, he gives himself over to sacrifice. Taking on suffering, he reminds them of the need to persevere when facing adversity. His willingness to undergo trials confronts them with their duty to rejoice. The vision of a re-created homeland lingers on the horizon.

KENNEY DOESN'T LIKE living in Newburgh. He calls its streets depressing, its people lacking in social graces, and its climate dismal. Having spent several years in Los Angeles on Skid Row at the Catholic Worker "hippie kitchen," he should know. Will we get stuck here, like Karen's mother, wandering the streets of Broadway collecting cans? Or will we end up like so many others who live here but whose hearts are somewhere else? Luanne's brother's words echo in my mind: "Everybody else left, thinking they were getting out of the Burg, but they all came back eventually, anyway. I just saved myself the trouble of leaving."

Friends like Aleyda made it possible for us to live in Newburgh, but only my husband and children made it a home. My greatest challenge, viewing the great, extending ring of community that we were privileged to enter, was to not confuse its *place* with its *source*. Like Aleyda, who lost her homeland and raises her children in another, I learned that while Newburgh holds the origin of memory, a geographical border cannot contain our future; salvation comes in the re-created Jerusalem — wherever that may be.

TWELVE YEARS AGO I visited the Basilica of the Virgin of Guadalupe in Mexico City as part of a Grail women's exchange. The others in the group had already entered the building; I hesitated, not quite prepared to lay eyes on her image. Roaming the congested streets around the Basilica, I was searching for an offering that would be worthy of this momentous meeting. The gift I had envisioned, conjured in my mind's eye by pure intuition, consisted of a bouquet of perfectly colored roses. Somehow I had decided they had to be pink and orange, a deep hue the color of sunset.

I lingered at the entrances of the many shops lining the streets of the Villa and explored the bowels of the complex where fancier shops offered pricier goods. Rosaries, replicas of the image, key rings, place mats, tiles, candles by the thousands — a dizzying array of souvenirs distracted me. Making my way to the flower stands where vendors sprayed shaded buckets of flowers to keep them from wilting in the scorching noonday sun, I searched for — but did not find — the right color roses.

When I was a child, my grandmother visited us in Newburgh with gifts she had bought at the Basilica. At the time of her trip we had questioned whatever possessed my grandmother — over seventy years old and never before having left the country — to make that pilgrimage. At the Basilica I thought of my grandmother, wondering what she thought of the swirling costumes of dancers in native costume, the huge *cazuelas* of rice and beans in the baking sun, and the brown-skinned image above the altar.

Just after her conversion and before she started the Catholic Worker, Dorothy Day too traveled to Mexico. She and her baby daughter lived with a family in Xochimilco, the green and flowering town now swallowed up by the sprawl of Mexico City, and visited the Basilica. Dorothy loved the people's religiosity and wrote that if her daughter hadn't kept getting sick, they might never have come back.

I never found the perfect-colored roses and pressed the ten thousand *peso* note, instead, into the begging hand of a barefoot old woman whose eyes were covered by white film and who wore a filthy, tattered green shawl. I knew, also by intuition, that while the Virgin loves flowers, she would prefer this offering to any bouquet. With certainty I heard her in the silence of my heart: if I wanted to give her something of real worth, my life for her children was all I could spend. Joining the young women already inside the Basilica, I laid eyes on the image that graced the altar with simple strength.

Our parish church in Newburgh too holds a larger-than-life image of the Virgin of Guadalupe. The Saturday after Janet's revelation, as Mass started, I acknowledged with a nod two young people I had taught, now catechists themselves. One of them still pines for her boyfriend, shot and killed in a gang-related incident a year ago; the other will be the first Mexican-American to graduate from the area's only Catholic high school. I also thought of Janet, who would not be here tonight. Eyes flickering over our own three children, who fidgeted restlessly on the seat beside us, I hoped they would make it through the service.

As I knelt for the consecration, my mind was flooded by thoughts that inundated my already-dampened spirit. How could my husband and I keep this crazy life in Newburgh together? Were we stretched too thin? Were we bringing in enough money? Did our efforts bear any fruit at all, or were they swept away by the never-ending stream of the city's woes?

I looked up, my eyes listlessly moving across the altar before they settled on a bouquet placed before the image of the Virgin of Guadalupe — a dozen peach-colored roses the hue of sunset. I did not need to "buy" her presence. She has been with me all along.

My salvation consists in exactly this: not the achieving, but rather the seeking to live out this offering's promise, close to the ones I love.

I USED TO THINK that if I could only decode the city's history, breaking apart the chapters of its decline, I could master it somehow — put a firm hand to steer my craft on these unruly waters and navigate my own way into its future. Covertly, I hoped to save the city from itself. Picturing myself as the loyal daughter who claims Newburgh for her own children's inheritance, I dreamed of ways to make it liveable.

One of my favorite quotes from Dorothy Day says, "Our job is not to look for results but to witness to the truth." I am a mother and a writer. I sit at the computer, when I wish I could be actively helping restore this breaking-down city. But as a disciple, I believe that only one thing is necessary. What brings me closest to an intimate relationship with Christ is writing, or rather, the silence from which it comes, flowering, like a night jasmine that needs the cool quiet to burst into fragrant flower, then is seen only as an imperceptible whiteness known by its sweet aroma —

a glowing in the dark that can serve as a landmark to memory, even as Dolly's roses once directed mine.

Writing for others I will never know, for one or two souls whose lives may be saved — as mine was saved by e.e. cummings and the Harlem Renaissance poets and Anna Akhmatova and Chaim Potok and Nztoke Shange and Simone Weil — becomes an act of faith. A believer who is also a writer must fling herself on the certainty that God — who has designed an interconnected universe in which the smallest particle of pollen on a single bee's leg fertilizes a field of corn that feeds many — will use this profligate use of time and energy called writing to nurture other souls in places to which I may never venture.

Instead of exploring new lands, I discovered a wealth of treasure in the hidden way, the way by which people have lived for thousands of years: tending children, planting gardens, showing neighborliness, and, by taking infinitesimal steps, changing the created world. As with St. Thérèse of Lisieux's "Little Way," so cherished by Dorothy, I found that small acts of faith mysteriously lead to redemption. Trusting that an unabashed love of beauty and inexplicable urge to tell the truth about my own inner life will lead to the Reign of God — even though I would much rather that God had made me a community organizer.

Remnant

Once a year each of the parish's committees plans a patronal feast to celebrate their countries of origin. The work begins months ahead. Coffee cans decorated with gift wrap and holy cards are set out in Latino stores and restaurants to take up a collection. Young people and children are set to practicing *bailables*, typical dances. Women on the committee argue about whether the dance steps are being done right; they sew folkloric costumes and deliberate about what foods to serve. Men discuss contracting professional musicians or deejays and organize the festivities' setup.

On the day itself, the Mass opens with a procession in which the flag of the country being celebrated is carried into the church and taken up to the altar. A statue or image, carefully arranged with flowers and streamers, is processed around the church building and then led up to take its rightful place — before the eyes of the whole people. Lectors from the country of origin have been sought to do the readings; the priest's homily will include a meditation on that country's particular image. The Peruvians in Newburgh celebrate the feast day of the Señor de los Milagros (the Lord of Miracles), who is special to the people of Lima. For most groups, however, images of the Virgin Mary symbolize their people's identity.

Like Mary in the Scriptures, who embodies the church of believers, these images express each people's deepest sorrows and loftiest aspirations. In line with — or because of this — intimacy, each group calls her by its own name for her. For Cubans, she is the "la Caridad del Cobre." For Dominicans, she is "Alta Gracia." For Hondurans, she is "la Virgen de Suyapa." For Puerto Ricans, she is "la Divina Providencia." For Mexicans, she is "la Virgen of Guadalupe."

In the parish gym after Mass, tables are laid out with foods. The walls and stage have been decorated with photos of beaches, mountains, and historic sites. Music (several decibels too loud) cranks out, cut off abruptly for announcements or speeches, and the party begins with the country of origin's national anthem. The *bailables* will be performed and folkloric songs sung.

For one day of the year, the young are immersed in their parents' culture. Never mind that their parents do not speak good English, that they perform jobs no one else wants to do, or that they have not found their way into the church the rest of the year. For this day, the church is *theirs*. Friends and relatives have driven in from New Jersey or Pennsylvania, from as far away as Virginia, to be here today. An exodus people weary of wandering in the desert catches a glimpse of home. The long years of exile — when one's language dries on the tongue, when one would give *anything* for a taste of comfort food, and when parents doubt their children will know their own history — come to a temporary reprieve. The same music their communities back home are listening to floods the gym. Dance steps rehearsed and re-rehearsed now find their enactment. Sustained for the journey, fed manna in the wilderness, they will continue their desert sojourn. But today, just this moment, there is home.

RUBY, WHOM I HAVE NOT SEEN since that last car ride to New Hampshire's frozen landscape twenty years ago, had a peculiar habit. Standing along the Bluff's grassy precipice, she would move her index finger slowly, methodically in a gesture of perfect concentration, her graceful figure poised in stillness save for that single extended fingertip. Lips pursed, she put all of her formidable energy into the padded fingertip rotating from a graceful wrist attached to a queenly arm that belonged to a body that was magnificent already, even for a fifteen-year-old. Yet her attention did not rest on the graceful finger moving hypnotically; her gaze settled on the horizon ahead, the beckoning of her life that would someday take her away from here. She was tracing the mountains, she explained, "just in case." When she moved away, she did not want to forget what they looked like.

I am reminded of Ruby's gesture as I contemplate my own internalized snapshots of the same river and mountains. Writing is never simply in an act of observation. Memory retained in the fingertips can chain or free. Maybe this narrative will free me from the mountain range where revolutionaries strung a freedom chain across the river.

Although I never saw her again, I know Ruby broke free. She left Newburgh for good and now works as a nurse practitioner farther north. She escaped the city, but its landscape travels with her. The rolling curves burned into the creases of her mind. The colors of a summer day, the mountains' deep green plush velour and the slight gray cast where the ridges run along, became part of her own vivacity. The size and shape and contours and even the smell became as familiar as a lover's shoulders. She was right to give them attention. Memorizing them against the day it would be time to leave.

THE FIRST TIME my young farmworker friend Rosa came to my house, we drove the river road from apple country into Newburgh. She was fifteen, the same age that Ruby and I were when I moved away. Originally from a farming village in one of Mexico's poorest states, then, more recently, from a *maquiladora* zone in the same state, Rosa had been here for only a few months. Without transportation, she was isolated in the farmworker camp and mostly stayed inside the trailer. She met with relief my offer to pick her up for a visit.

As we approached Newburgh along the road running parallel to the river's banks, Rosa watched the river's waves dance in the sunshine. She took in a view of Bannerman's Island with its ruined castle to the right, the bridge with its artful design to the left. As I turned onto Broadway toward our house, we drove past magnificent, crumbling mansions; the city's impressive library; the pillared Dutch Reformed church, which, once again, a community group has reclaimed for a cultural center. Rosa was speechless. *"Su pueblo está muy bonito"* ("Your town is very pretty"), she finally breathed. A thousand responses cluttered my head.

Should I tell her how I spent my childhood growing up here? Should I explain to her about drugs, or crime? Should I summarize for her a brief history of immigrants to the Hudson Valley, or remind her that this land was taken from the Native Americans? I carefully considered my answer, and then turned and simply told her: she was right. I know — I have glimpsed both its internal and its external beauty.

Newburgh needs social workers, and teachers, and pastoral workers, and organic gardeners, and nutritionists, and counselors. Maybe even more it needs community organizers, activists, agitators. I am none of those things. A writer and a theologian, a wife and mother, I am simply, inexcusably, inescapably, and imperfectly: a witness. My own corner of the city flourished in a jungle-like garden, bursting at the seams. I have fed my children on its bounty, and I have introduced them to the perfect proportion of mountain, water, and sky found only at this particular bend of the Hudson River Valley.

My remembered landscape painted a picture of perfect proportions of sky and land reflected on the water's smooth veneer — illusions of a permanence that does not exist. Appearances of tranquility betray the many struggles that have taken place — and *are* taking place — on its banks. I have introduced our children to these struggles, too. The water, however, is neutral: like liquid glass its wide gray body ripples out toward both shores, refusing to choose sides but ever stretching... reaching... flowing out to embrace both. Stunningly beautiful and invisibly toxic, the waters kiss the banks with a familiarity hundreds of thousands of years old. That the mountains and river will outlive us all, the many tribes who people these banks, is not what awes me. It is the mindless brilliance with which they will outlast us. Neither for us nor against us, they are not indifferent, either. Housing some chamber of memory, they whisper a symphony of music: warriors' death chants, settlers' tall tales, immigrants telling their children about the old country, border-crossing stories and music in abundance for all with ears to hear. Offering a lap of familiarity — if not comfort — the wide-hipped mountains with the lapping river at their feet beckon all who would listen to come home.

ONE SPRING DAY last year I found myself giving a retreat on the Virgin of Guadalupe to some forty Mexican adults (and surely just as many children). After the session and a meal, we walked in procession, carrying the sacred image from the meeting room to the chapel building, singing the songs I recognize from seven years of *mañanitas* (early morning serenades) on December 12 and scores of Masses at the farmworker camps.

It was the exodus journey: a weary march through streets all too familiar, a wilderness to be endured (with all its danger and futility) year after year. But this was a homecoming, too. An arrival to the land for which exiles yearn: a homeland, an inheritance. When viewed properly, the desert wasteland of Newburgh finds its expression in the lush verdant beauty of summer. A city of sojourners surrounded by wooded areas, bordered by farmland north and south, it welcomes newcomers to the fertile banks of the most beautiful river in the world.

The priest gave a running homily as we walked.

"We are walking back to the South from the North. We are walking back home. We are going to our real home, to our heavenly home. You thought you came here to earn dollars. But God had a plan of which you were not aware. You came here to bring guadalupanismo *to this country, which needs to hear its message. Your life here has a purpose. You think you chose to come here, but it was not your choice that brought you. Now that you are here without papers, you think you cannot choose to go back. But there is One greater than you who already has your home prepared. 'In my father's house there are many rooms.' And when you find yourself far from home, having worked hard for people who think that's all you're good for, and when you have spent every ounce of strength you have, and when you have given your life over for your children without knowing how they will turn out, give thanks. How good. You will know how it is to end up with your arms outstretched, like this, in the shape of the cross."*

It was then that I knew I could leave. Sooner or later, I will leave. This procession is not mine. And yet, this procession, this church are mine insofar as I have walked this path. The people with whom I have walked will — because they *must* — find their way. I have been a fellow pilgrim, a sister *guadalupana*, a teacher and a friend. I am a *madrina* and a *comadre*. I am not one of them, even though I have shared this path. There will be other paths — all of them exodus journeys.

My husband walks by my side; Rachel, Thomas, and Seamus (the only blonds in the straggling line of children) keep pace with us. I belong to them, and they to me. I reach for my husband's hand; it is dry and strong and firm. He responds to my timid touch by grasping not only my hand but my arm as well. The path that brought me back here is the same one that will someday take me away from here. We have many landscapes to explore, some here, and others elsewhere. The river and mountains and sky in perfect proportion travel with me, engraved into my being. But there will be other rivers and other mountains under the same sky. Our exodus will continue, together, and our exile will come to an end, forever. It is good. It is finished.

> *Seek the Lord while the Lord may be found,*
>   *call upon God while God is near . . .*
> *For as the rain and the snow come down from heaven,*
>   *and do not return there until they have watered the earth,*
> *making it bring forth and sprout,*
>   *giving seed to the sower and bread to the eater,*
> *so shall my word be that goes out from my mouth;*
>   *it shall not return to me empty,*
> *but it shall accomplish that which I purpose,*
>   *and succeed in the thing for which I sent it.*
> *For you shall go out in joy,*
>   *and be led back in peace;*
> *the mountains and the hills before you*
>   *shall burst into song.*

— Isaiah 55